Editorial

AI developers have perpetrated an immense piracy on writers of all shapes and sizes, and indeed on digitally archived magazines and journals. They feed the words into text digestion- and regurgitation-programmes so that students and larger pirates (including front-bench politicians) can present us with by-products of our work.

The issue of 'copyright clearance' may seem to pale into insignificance beside such technological voracity. But for the author, critic, anthologist, journalist, it is a disagreeable, time-consuming task and it can be very expensive. In her book *Also a Poet*, centring on her and her father's relations with the life of Frank O'Hara, Ada Calhoun quotes six lines from Auden's 'In Memory of W.B. Yeats', published in 1940. She would have preferred to quote the whole poem, as her father had, but

> for permission to share these six lines I had to sign two contracts and pay $285.37. So for the rest, please look up the poem free on the Internet and imagine it being read in the top-floor kitchen of an East Village brownstone by a very thin man with a scraggly beard while his middle-aged daughter, looking tired, her hair in a ponytail, leans against the counter and listens.

Maybe we should be grateful because the licensing process did elicit a vivid and wry paragraph from the author, and the fact of the *magnitude* of the fee will surprise and alert some readers. As William Carlos Williams's UK publisher, I always contend that 'So much depends / upon' is less about a red wheelbarrow, more about the importance of copyright fees in the ecology of poetry publishing.

Clearance is required for re-use – in books, anthologies, articles for this journal, even memorial addresses – of material copyrighted and printed, though much of it exists gratis (by mistake or by deliberate piracy) online. Copyright does expire and work eventually enters the public domain, but its quotation always carries a whiff of danger: has the passage quoted been re-edited, so that copyright is restored for an additional period, as with the writings of D.H. Lawrence and Charlotte Mew? Was it published posthumously, so that copyright starts with the date of first publication? *Caveat scriptor*. Some authors and their agencies and estates patrol the wynds and snickets of contemporary writing armed and ready to strike.

Another kind of authority, exercised less for pelf and more for narrative control, resides with estates who see it as their duty to police the posthumous reputation of the writers whose executors they are. Readers can be entirely unaware of how much is withheld, and why. Again, copyright will expire and eventually the beans will all be spilled (if an appetite for those beans, and the typescripts, survive). The censorship of a literary legacy can affect the reception of the writer's work. Issues of politics, sexuality and other elements can be kept under wraps. Many a literary scholar comes up against such barriers. Some may know the truth but are not permitted to disclose it. The whole truth can be more telling, more to the author's credit, than the protection of well-meaning guardians. Relatively minor indiscretions can blur and erase a writer's large discretions. Even if their statues are not tumbled into Bristol Harbour, their works can be removed to storerooms, their books withdrawn from circulation in bookshops and libraries...

Other more personal, small-scale acts of censorship blur the record. When Philip Larkin's letters were being edited, I was approached for permission to print a few disobliging things he had said in letters about Carcanet and about me. I agreed: it was part of the record and I respect archival completeness, though I was sad that this man, courteous and wry in person, was far from courteous in private correspondence. A close friend of the poet was approached at the same time for permission to quote. He refused: the passages about him did not appear. There was no indication of what or who had been omitted from the final volume.

Letter to the editor

Nicolas Jacobs writes: Sam Adams suggests ('Letter from Wales', *PNR* 273) that Waldo Williams's choice of the title *Dail Pren* (Leaves of the Tree) for the only collection of his poems published in his lifetime may have been in part inspired by the title of Walt Whitman's *Leaves of Grass*. That can hardly be disproved, but a much more obvious source is surely Revelation 22:2, which reads in English, 'In the midst of the street of it, and on either side of the river, was there the tree of life, which bare twelve manner of fruits, and yielded her fruit every month: and the leaves of the tree were for the healing of the nations' (*a daily pren oedd I iacháu'r cenhedloedd*). The text continues, 'And there shall be no more curse'. This would fit perfectly with Waldo's commitment to pacifism, which underpins so much of his best poetry.

Yours ever
Nicolas Jacobs

News & Notes

Louise Glück • *John McAuliffe writes:* Louise Glück's remarkable poems have been published in Great Britain across her entire writing life, initially by Anvil and, since 1996, by Carcanet. It has been a recurring pleasure at Carcanet to publish her for three decades.

Greeting her classic 1996 collection *The Wild Iris*, Helen Vendler caught something of her poetry's fierce, brilliant independence: 'Louise Glück is a poet of strong and haunting presence. Her poems, published in a series of memorable books over the last twenty years, have achieved the unusual distinction of being neither "confessional" nor "intellectual" in the usual senses of those words, which are often thought to represent two camps in the life of poetry'.

Glück would continue to steer that original path through the great books that followed, including *Averno* and *A Village Life* and, most recently, her first, fable-like fiction, *Marigold and Rose* (2022), as well as *Winter Recipes from the Collective* (2021).

In her essay 'The Education of the Poet', Glück wrote, 'The dream of art is not to assert what is already known but to illuminate what has been hidden'. For half a century, Glück listened hard for hidden voices and found images which speak both to personal crises and perennial mysteries, an endeavour recognised in 2020 by the award of the Nobel Prize in Literature. The citation declared, 'if Glück would never deny the significance of the autobiographical background, she is not to be regarded as a confessional poet. Glück seeks the universal, and in this she takes inspiration from myths and classical motifs, present in most of her works.'

One of this candid poet's most striking lines, from her poem 'Nostos', a Greek word for homecoming, speaks to the astonishing recoveries her poems enact for her readers: 'We look at the world once, in childhood. The rest is memory.'

Alongside the 2020 Nobel Prize, her other awards include the National Humanities Medal, the Pulitzer Prize, the National Book Award, the Bollingen Prize, the Wallace Stevens Award from the Academy of American Poets and the Gold Medal for Poetry from the American Academy of Arts and Letters.

Daisy Fried writes: I hear that Louise Glück has died. A Great poet, great with a capital G. I knew her a little (not well at all) and my own writing, and sense of myself as a poet, are the better for this, and certainly because of her work.

It's funny to think of how as a very young woman I didn't understand Glück's austerities – young people often don't read well across temperamental differences, and I was no exception. But I began to learn what it was about her as I grew up a little. Her rigour, her astonishments. Over the years I've read her pretty constantly and taught her often, especially *Meadowlands* and, last year, her last book of poems, *Winter Recipes from the Collective.* When she won the Nobel, I thought: 'oh, yes, perfect'.

I first met her when *American Poetry Review* brought her to Philadelphia to give a master class, a class for high school teachers, a reading and a lecture. I was in that master class. She only workshopped three poems out of the ten submitted by the ten members of the workshop. She said that she thought it was more valuable for all of us if she went deeply into a few poems, rather than run superficially over all of the poems – and she was right. My husband Jim's was one of the poems she workshopped in class. She invited everyone else to make an appointment to meet with her during the week she was in town. Obviously I took her up on this. She gave me interesting advice that I believe I didn't end up taking – but it was smart advice. It was just that I decided I had different aims from those that advice was aimed at. This too taught me something about conversations about poems, how there can be all kinds of good advice but you have to discover in it your own aims and your own temperament. She also told me that if I revised the poem I could send it to her. I remember that she said she did not promise to write back to me about it but she did promise to read it. This too was important to me: that honesty, that clear giving and also giving of boundaries. I doubt she ever bullshitted anyone ever. That's rare in the poetry world, and something to emulate. She was quite well known and in demand by then, and this was a big generosity.

A little while after that, I entered a first book prize she judged, and did not win, but apparently was one of a handful of people she wrote to after the prize. What she said to me: that I had come close but that she didn't think the book was quite ready yet. She was, of course, right, and as a result I revised and cut and added. The next year my book did win a publication prize.

Final anecdote. The *Threepenny Review*, where she'd been publishing for years, and where by then I'd also published several times, was having an anniversary party in New York City, and I went to it. Perhaps I was living in Princeton that year, on the Hodder. She was reading at the party. So was Robert Pinsky, I recall. I remember him reading a poem by Thom Gunn. Maybe Thom had just died. I'm not sure. Anyway at the after party, I was feeling rather like a junior member of the poetry world, quite shy, and I remember Robert lifting up Louise's coat to put it on her shoulders and while he was doing that, Louise spotting me halfway across the room and calling out 'Daisy Fried, your poems are getting so good!' That was it, but that was when I felt like I was a real poet and it put me at ease.

These are not very significant stories. I remember going to her readings a number of times, and one particular Q&A, maybe at Bryn Mawr, when she gave some advice about revision, wherein she said that with drafts she wasn't happy with sometimes she would take the ending of the draft and put it in the middle of the poem and then keep on writing from there. This blew my head off, poets. I've passed that suggestion along (with credit) ever since. It doesn't always work, but it often does.

That's all. I'm so sorry her voice is now silent.

Poundian • Michael Alexander, the poet, Poundian and major scholar of old English, died in October. Until his retirement, he was a Professor of English Literature at St Andrews University. He translated the Penguin Classics *Beowulf*, edited *The Earliest English Poems* and *The Canterbury Tales: The First Fragment*. His critical study *The Poetic Achievement of Ezra Pound* won a Scottish Arts Council Book Award. He also wrote *A History of Old English Literature* and *Medievalism: The Middle Ages in Modern England*. For Anvil Press he translated the *Old English Riddles*, the secular portion of the celebrated *Exeter Book*. This is number forty-five:

> I have heard of something hatched in a corner:
> It thrusts, rustles, raises its hat.
> A bride grabbed at that boneless thing,
> Handled it proudly: a prince's daughter
> Covered that swelling creature with her robe.

It is hard to work out the answer to number seventy-five: 'I saw a woman sit alone'. Most readers will have worked out that number forty-five is not what it seems to be. It will finally turn into a loaf but at this stage it is – dough.

Diego Roel • The Argentinian poet Diego Roel has received the thirty-sixth Loewe Award for Poetry – one of the most significant international awards for poetry – for his book *Los cuadernos perdidos de Robert Walser* (*The lost notebooks of Robert Walser*). It is a generous prize, of €30,000, and it received 2,302 submissions from forty-four countries, the bulk of them from Spain and Latin America. Roel's book draws on German, French and English Romantic literature, Walser being the qualifier and unifier of what the judges described as an exceptionally consistent and coherent single work. The lost notebook form manages to bring together elements of epistle, *pensée*, reflection, and fragments that recall haikus.

The Y • 92NY, the 92nd Street Y, has 'paused' (temporarily halted) its literary series, having cancelled an event by an author critical of Israel. 92NY has been one of the key literary resources for international and new American writing. They pulled the event with Pulitzer Prize-winning novelist Viet Thanh Nguyen out of concern over his public comments. The event took place in a bookshop in downtown Manhattan, without the Y's involvement. As a result, several writers scheduled to speak at the Y withdrew, and some of the staff of the Unterberg Poetry Center (which has hosted writers including Dylan Thomas, Robert Frost, Langston Hughes, Philip Roth, Salman Rushdie and Toni Morrison) resigned. Unfortunate timing: 92NY is celebrating its 150th anniversary – having been founded as the Young Men's Hebrew Association, its mission to serve 'the social and spiritual needs of the American Jewish community'.

On Hold • *Poetry* magazine, in Chicago, sent out an anonymous message on 2 November to 'Our Communities', 'In response to discussions around a recent editorial decision'. The language used is unspecific, cautious, neutral, attempting to disappear into the news it is revealing and concealing at the same time. Clearly a committee, or AI pretending to be a committee, is responsible for the pious drafting. 'We at the Poetry Foundation are saddened and deeply disturbed by the humanitarian crisis and ongoing violence in Palestine and Israel. While we believe in the power of words to transform lives, it is not a practice of the Poetry Foundation to insert itself when it cannot add to the conversation or may divert attention away from the work being done by those directly impacted and involved.' Then we get to the meat of the matter. 'Staff' (no names, because 'staff' is nameless) 'had scheduled a review of a poetry collection to be published on October 9, which included a discussion of the reviewer's and poet's identities as anti-Zionist Jewish writers. Because of the events that began on October 7, a decision was made' (note the passive voice) 'in the immediate aftermath to postpone publication to be sensitive to those directly impacted by the violence and avoid exposing both writers to potential backlash. Staff' (again) 'informed the review author' (who also remains anonymous) 'that we would put the piece on hold temporarily, to which they initially agreed; as conversations with the author continued, they informed us that they would be withdrawing the piece and pitching it elsewhere. We respect the author's decision, and let them know that they could proceed as they wished.' Having clearly suppressed an item intended for publication, the statement goes on to declare that, 'The Poetry Foundation does not censor poets or dictate what topics they might discuss while writing for, recording with, or performing at the Foundation. It's unfortunate that this was how the interactions were interpreted and that it generated misinformation and misunderstandings within our communities.' It is reassuring to learn that 'We at the Poetry Foundation' (staff?) 'will continue to uplift work being done by those who raise their voices against oppression. We maintain our mission to foster spaces for all to create, experience, and share poetry, and we are grounded by our values of sharing, collaboration, equity, access, innovation, and growth.' Uplift, foster spaces for all (with certain exceptions). The public statement is signed by 'The Poetry Foundation'.

Funding Crisis • Several literary magazines have reported difficulties around funding. *The White Review*, co-founded by publisher Jacques Testard, announced in September that it would 'go on indefinite hiatus' because Arts Council funding had not been awarded. The author Julia Armfield declared, '*The White Review* was astonishingly important to me and to so many other writers at the beginning of our careers and throughout'. *Bad Form*, run by Amy Mae Baxter, announced last month that it would cease online publication. Baxter told the *Guardian*: 'The UK's literary magazine scene is crumbling due to rising print costs. I had to announce that I couldn't do it any more. The cost of printing magazines has grown astronomically. The cost of Royal Mail postage to ship the print issues has gone up. Even X, formerly known as Twitter, has announced its plans to start charging us to use its service, which would be a critical blow.' The *Cardiff Review* announced its demise in October and *Gal-Dem* – after eight years – folded its tent last April. Our days are numbered...

Reports

Fire & Darkness

And Also / No Join / Like

ANTHONY VAHNI CAPILDEO

Read at the Rylands Poetry Reading marking the *PN Review* Jubilee, 19 October 2023

'O Love, that fire and darkness should be mix'd,
Or to thy triumphs such strange torments fix'd!'
– John Donne, 'Elegy XIII'

A northern street: the temperature of the ungovernable. The proud hooded stride. The skill to add up stone: cold – outlasting. The wealth of the land: stone. Kindness: the harsh kind. For each question, a better question. For each better question, one answer. For each good question – that'll do. Not fussed.

I walk the hollow walk: loving more than loved; moved, scarce more than moving.

> and also

In the south of this country, five times I have attended the celebrations that they hold in the dark of the year. Many centuries ago, there was a man whose name was Guy, or Guido. He practised a different, competing version of the national religion. He tried to explode an important government site. These buildings are still in use. You can visit the place, which is on the river. Some of the children who ask for money on British streets are simply trying to fund their construction of effigies of this hate figure, whose burning on public and domestic pyres on the so-called 'Bonfire Night' (5 November) has become a popular ritual. Fireworks are let off; it is legal to purchase them for your own festivities.

> no join

A northern street, uphill. It branches, like – a Y, a peace sign, water coursing round an outcrop; like – part of the net of a tree; like – it branches in two. Upon the slope held between the branches stands a sooty church, now in use as a nightclub. This pale and brisk morning glances on the metal railings.

Who is he?
Nobody.
Who is he, between the fence and lamp post?
Nobody. A hat stuck on the railing, abandoned by a tidy drunk. A feeble visual joke. Nobody's head, nobody's, supports a hat drooped at that angle.

It is a guy. A Guy Fawkes guy. The students left him there: lad for the burning: unreal, it has to be unreal. Check out this guy.

I have to cross the road, so I do.

The ordinary-looking foot is wedged between the base of the fence and the lamp post. The left arm, bent at the elbow, has been tucked deep into the jacket pocket, toneless. It is not a bad face. The eye is the pity of it: tender lids tightened into a crescent, as happens with mortally wounded birds; infolding, no longer able to yield, a turning inwards of the ability to light up.

I put my hand into my pocket, for my phone.

It is not necessary.

Pale and brisk as this morning, the police car slides into my peripheral vision.

> and also

A street in Trinidad: the soft, brown 'ground doves' have the same manners as the pedestrians. Unhurried, they traipse along in front of cars. Why did the ground dove cross the road? I don't know, but it's certainly taking its time.

The exception came plummeting out of the recessive sky, into the back yard's concrete rain gutter. Had a neighbourhood boy felled it inexpertly? Had the ecstatic efficiency of its heart thumped to a stop? It lay there, the softness, and would not, could not bestir itself.

The child strewed it with yellow and scarlet wild lantana flowers, thinking of burial, accustomed to cremation; feeling a sudden fear. The parents took it all away.

And when the dove was gone, another came plummeting the same way; the riddle repeated — to be moved, moving, and never to move. Love or some other force was identical in the equation.

> no join

We brought few friends home who were not already part of at least a two-generation family circle. We brought few friends home. This time my brother had introduced a soft and brown and tallish young man in his early twenties, who weighed not much more than a hundred pounds. By historical pattern, not personal choice, in our secular Hindu household, this was the first Muslim friend our age.

Perhaps it has changed; but non-Indo-Caribbeans used not to be aware that 'Ali' and 'Mohammed' are not 'Indian' names. And in that unawareness they are linguistically wrong, but more profoundly right: for our ancestors brought over a shared Indian village culture, over a century before the creation of Pakistan in the Indus area made such a difference. And in that Trinidad remote from Trinidad's Trinidad, and nonetheless most mixed and Trinidadian, a lunatic reverberation was set up by the 1947 Partition – some third-generation immigrant families briefly fought according to the lines of what had not been a division. In lands far away, current events were indirectly regenerating or inventing this part of Trinidad's past also. By 1990, we knew that there must be some difference. We sat on the nice imported sofa with the delicate novel unicorn visitant who looked just like us.

All over the island, every evening just before seven, telephone calls were wound down, fires turned low beneath pots, and families converged on the television set to listen to the news headlines: a link with the greater world. Nothing was expected to happen.

A square, reliable face showed up.

'The liberation of Kuwait has begun.'

The look of devastation and betrayal on our guest's face was like nothing I could have imagined seeing. An outline seemed to be sitting in his place, while the person who had occupied that outline crumbled.

Why? Televised missile fireworks were going off, white and purple. What had so upset him?

I tried to see with his eyes. Brownskinned people with strong features and children of adorable gravity were being killed from the air; and en masse they looked more like us than anyone else on television, local or international, in those days. My insides flipped. People who looked like they could be family were being killed from the air.

We are not evolved to cope with aerial threats. To witness the spectacle of bombing is to feel guilty and due to be wiped out; for all our gods inhabit the heavens, and to be safe our earliest kind might have taken to the trees, where only the gods could smite them. To be bombed is to be smitten by the wrath of a deity not to be located and not in our image. To ascend into Heaven becomes profoundly and secretly inconceivable; for the borders of the heavens are guarded with fire.

Was this what our friend was seeing? The starring roles in war, in our young memories, hitherto had been for people who did not look like us. Or was he seeing war upon his religion?

From now on, anyway, in the world's play of representations of the living, we would look more like the killed. We would resemble – like it or not – anti-advertisements for flourishing societies; which is perhaps why people on the street in the south of England have told me that they have no money, or have offered me money, when I have said nothing or when I was about to ask for directions and certainly have not had a guy to burn.

Our soft brown young man sat, and sat, until he could get himself home.

no join

no join

no join

and also

like

like

like

Mondo de Kvar Anguloj (World of Four Corners)

translated by

JOHN GALLAS

1. Mondo de arboj

In coming issues of *PN Review*, John Gallas will contribute to the 'Reports' pages five-poem anthologies of translations from many corners of the world. He is, after all, the author of *The Song Atlas*. Esperanto provides our titles going forward. The next five are proposed as:

2. Mondo de mašino
3. Mondo de dormo
4. Mondo de sunbrilo
5. Mondo de melankolio
6. Mondo de birdoj

MONDO DE ARBOJ

1
Three Trees

Gabriela Mistral 1889–1957/Chile

Three fallen trees
just left at the side of the path.
The woodcutter forgot them, and they are talking together,
woodily, about love, like three blind men.

The setting sun lays
its lifeblood on the chopped logs,
and the breeze carries away the sweet smell
of their opened flanks.

The crookedest one reaches out
its huge arm and shivered leaves
towards the others, and its wounds,
like two eyes, are full of entreaty.
The woodcutter forgot them. Night
will come. I will stay with them.
I will welcome into my heart their gentle
sap. They will be like a fire to me.

2
I wonder, how you will manage...

Princess Ōku 661–702/Japan

I wonder, how you will manage
to cross the mountains all alone,
in autumn, in the darkness of the fading trees,
and the shortening days.

Even when we went,
the two of us together,
when the forest was green, and the long days light,
I remember it was difficult enough.

3
Death of old men

Anonymous/Côte d'Ivoire

Old Henri is dying. Children play tag in the dust.
And we, whose world is next, sit with him under the tree
and watch his knowledge burn:
All he said – like a dictionary
All he did – like an atlas
All he was – like a library...

Old Henri is dying. Youngsters fight in the grass.
And we, whose haul is next, sit with him under the tree
and watch his knowledge burn:
All he thought – like an encyclopaedia
All he imagined – like a storybook
All he was – like a library...

4
The Plum Tree
Bertolt Brecht 1898–1956/Germany

There's a Plum Tree in the square, so skinny it's hardly there.
Round about it has a little picket, so no one can kick it.

And though it wants to blossom, oh, so very much, it
    just can't grow.
The few hours' sun are not much use: the sun can't
    reproduce.

The little tree that's hardly there, whose little life looks
    black and brief,
is still a Plum Tree, though it's bare – because it has a
    Plum Tree's leaf.

5
To a silly Lord who cut off his potboy's hair when drunk
Abul Qasim Unsuri d.1039/40 Persia

So you regret, sir, that you cut off his hair.
Such is drink. Well, that was last night.
Why worry? Cheers. Bottoms up. Who cares?
Every little tree in your garden looks better trimmed.

Unfacts

J. KATES

'Thus the unfacts, did we possess them, are too imprecisely few to warrant our certitude.'
James Joyce, *Finnegans Wake*

In her later life, my mother occasionally reminisced about the friends of her earlier years, often without naming them. More than once, she spoke of letters she had received from a young man she had known in her college years. From Paris, he had written to her about visiting James Joyce's *atelier*. When I asked what had become of his letters, as they might be of interest to Joyce scholars, she replied almost too quickly, 'Oh, they're lost now'. She answered so readily and so definitively that I guessed her correspondent had meant more to her than she let on. Perhaps he was identical with a young man she talked about who had fought and died in the Spanish Civil War, and perhaps she was positive the letters were lost because she herself had destroyed them.

Unfacts indeed. We were both wrong on most counts. After my mother's death in late 2011, a cache of letters written to her during her high-school and college years came to light. Many were from her two older brothers – one a law student at Harvard, the other a medical student in Edinburgh – giving her insight into family dynamics and advice about how to live in the world. One letter included a news clipping about a raid on a speakeasy in 1931, Julius's Village Café, which is active to this day at the same address in Greenwich Village – as a gay bar now. There were also letters from a former English teacher, an older woman recommending André Gide to her and particularly concerned when my mother almost died of typhoid fever at summer camp. It was the same camp where she had become acquainted with one of the counsellors, a young theatrical aspirant, Cliff Odets, who directed the camp black-face minstrel shows. (We have the playbills.)

And there were letters from suitors, college boys falling all over themselves trying to express their ardour and show off their erudition, sounding as if they had fallen out of the pages of *This Side of Paradise*. One of these was Reuben Goldberg, 'Ruby', who graduated from the University of Pennsylvania in 1931 and then travelled to France, but who had been courting my mother at least since 1928 (when she was fifteen years old), writing in such terms as 'You'll have to excuse every-part of this letter Because I think I'm awfully in love – with you. And you probably know how silly one acts when one thinks that he one is in love..' In 1930, his 'favorite poets right now & besides a permanent like for John Gould Fletcher, are Li-Po and Tu-Fu – also Chang Wow Kien'.

And then in a letter postmarked July 27, 1932, this:

Oh! such festees, & such excites. Must we hide behind the inkstlained thombgue. Listme. Having returned to Paris, greeted by a bevy of letters, of which yours head-headeth... [my ellipses]
Went out last night & between Dome, Corysol, Scribe Bar, Rouzers Perigordine & others through

which I must return to answer charges. Was over at Jimmy Joyces workshop yesterday afternoon. Bought explifation of Factafication of something 'of' Work in Progress. Very amusing, being detailed accounts of what JJ's trying to do – seems he's going back to Vecco and rehabilitating neglected philosophy of history, doctoring it up in the words of any language or if no word exact, making of them in Jabberwocky style, removing the whole out of time, & so writing it, as not to be writing about a certain thing, but *writing it*. Very clearly arranged & things simplethuse. Also some of Eliots vague far off cacklings. Have decided to shun Sorbonne & study art stead –...

I set this letter beside an anecdote related in 'Silence, Exile, Punning: James Joyce's Chance Encounters' by Louis Menand, in *The New Yorker*, 2 July 2002, pp. 72–3:

In 1932, two young Americans, Dwight Macdonald and George Morris, recent Yale graduates with an interest in modern literature and art, were in Paris, where they bought a copy of 'Ulysses,' still outlawed in the United States, at the English-language bookstore Shakespeare and Company. They got into a conversation with the owner, Sylvia Beach, the woman who had published 'Ulysses,' and she arranged for them to meet Joyce. They showed up at Joyce's apartment and plied him eagerly with questions about his work. He was unresponsive. 'It was like trying to open a safe without the combination,' Macdonald later said. Finally, one of them made a remark about people not knowing what to do with their lives. Joyce suddenly perked up. He gestured toward a window. 'There are people who go walkin' up and down the street,' he said, 'and they don't know what they want.'

The July 1932 letter was the last from Ruby Goldberg. It was difficult to learn what became of him, a young man who may have passed Macdonald and Morris in the stairwell or walkin' up and down the street. When we first tried to look him up on the internet, we stumbled over too many references to his better known namesake, Rube Goldberg, the fantastic cartoonist of improbable machinery. More recently, we think we've found a record of him as a creative museum photographer who died in 1960.

After 1933, we have no letters in my mother's collection until those from her children twenty and thirty years later. In 1935, she married my father, a rising New York businessman, on the day before his thirty-first birthday. They separated in 1957, and were divorced in 1958. To the end of her life, I am not sure she knew what she wanted. I certainly hope Ruby did.

Postcard from Taiwan

MILES BURROWS

At the herb-garden restaurant, outside on the grass, the people at the next table ask X

– *How old is he?*

– *Kon Long* (dinosaur), replies X.

That is usually enough. They are asking out of friendly curiosity.

I have a slight tremor of the left hand, which makes me seem more decrepit. I could conceal it by putting the arm in a sling as if it is some sporting injury. (*Guardi le stelle, che tremano d'amore.*) T tells me not to hunch my shoulder and to keep my head back and not to adopt a sarcastic expression.

– Englishmen's lips are not shaped in a way to catch bits of noodle falling onto their chin. They are only well shaped to make sarcastic remarks.

The restaurant is set in the middle of a field planted with medicinal trees and shrubs. Other diners are in groups, in T-shirts, with children. We look round the garden, and go into the canteen where the herbs are displayed and labelled and we can choose which we like for our meal. Then we choose the beans, chicken and freshly picked lemon grass, then go to our trestle table, where each place has a hot pot (*huo-guo*) set into the table, and a kind of individual dashboard under the table, allowing each adult and even child to adjust the time and temperature to cook his dish.

X is happy because he has been caring for at least fourteen abandoned cats from a disused railway station at Shang-Li. He is a retired engineer. He has been travelling twenty miles every week to feed the cats at the disused station with tinned cat food from the supermarket. He first decided to adopt a tortoiseshell cat named *Heido* (little black bean). She was tiny like a rat and always bullied by the other cats and could only get leftovers. She developed a skill to catch snakes because she was always so hungry. Heido and Miki are the only two completely adopted and resident. Heido is shy but comes forward to be patted round the backside affectionately. Miki is nowhere to be seen but takes up positions of safety on a high shelf or somewhere out of sight where he can spring down.

In the railway stations, in the supermarkets, at all times of day and night gleaming shiny white ceramic tiles are being polished by girls with yellow or orange small head-scarves to protect their hair, using mops attentively, proudly. Lovingly, going back time and again if one tile is not so shiny.

In the bullet train, a girl is going up and down pushing a trolley to collect rubbish. It's the same in the underground supermarkets, which are quiet, without music or constant announcements and new offers, and there's another girl happily polishing the mirror-shiny white floors, which look like white marble. And even, in the heart of the supermarket, a bench where you can just sit down.

T's nephew, a policeman, once came to England and was impressed by the English underground, especially by the announcement 'MIND THE GAP'. This gap has still not been closed by successive architects over a hundred years, and so the announcement is still made today. This surprised him. In Taiwan they have a seamless underground system, fast, quiet and clean, and not the slightest gap or step. And still, as if in commemoration of the Edwardian tube, they always make their own announcement in Chinese and English: MIND THE GAP.

After breakfast, like clockwork, Indonesian carers push old people in wheelchairs under the tree affectionately as the abandoned cats they have adopted.

Tsi-tsun means dignity, self-respect, face.

– Stand up straight and smile. Not hunched up like an old person.

The noise of the *Maiden's Prayer*, piano music composed by a Polish girl dying of tuberculosis at the age of eighteen more than a hundred years ago, is now blaring out from mobile refuse trucks every evening, to signal they are coming. Householders (who are unlikely to be thinking about this music) quickly gather up their day's rubbish and stand outside their houses waiting for the garbage truck to pass by.

'No rubbish to touch the ground', is the government's slogan.

All the houses are defended by a stout metal door to the front garage-space and then by at least two inner doors, set behind each other in the one doorway. The first door is a metal mosquito net, and the inner one is a heavy solid steel door such as you might expect in the vault of a bank. This metal grid mosquito screen has its own lock and should only be opened for a moment to prevent mosquitos entering. It's no good opening it and then wondering where the next key is. This (if you have the key) gives access to the heavy inner door of solid steel.

Fortification is repeated at the windows. In a four-storey block, each house will have its windows protected by a grille of metallic bars. These are shining stainless steel, slim and close together. A huge metal water barrel shines on every rooftop. Seen *en masse* from a passing train going by a street near the railway, you have the impression of a set of cages for rare birds, or hutches for expensive and precious jumping mice. The buildings present a mixture of Spanish with toy-town, with red-roofed turrets and balconies.

In front of the door all you can see is a row of different sandals, about ten pairs, and each pair pointing neatly towards you (outwards from the double house-door). But when you do get to open the outermost of the double doors (I am still trapped in the garage-space) you take off your outdoor slippers inside this door and put on a pair of indoor slippers waiting for you inside, in its own kind of intermediate space, on the step. All the slippers, too, are pointing outwards. You also should be pointing outwards away from the house while entering, out of respect. You enter backwards.

Camouflage sandals, blue elastic fitting canvas, white plastic with toe-catchers, grey-blue strapovers, Zohar Italian, pink plimsolls, blue, grey and red gym shoes, blue perforated-sole slipovers, blue slipover sports, blue slip-ons with bubbly soles. Remember which are yours.

Before dawn at 4.30 am, to avoid the heat, we cycle along dark alleys decorated with pots of flowers and mango trees, up the cycle track to the temple hill and the morning market. On the temple hill it is important not to go too near the memorial tablets of soldiers who died in the China–Japan war, where ghosts are wandering about. And to avoid the still half damaged grassy concrete underground Japanese air-raid shelters where undesirables could be hiding for the night with knives hidden in their sleeping bags.

Halfway up the hill there is tango music from loudspeakers and people aged mainly around sixty or so are dancing on a flat arena. Another group are bending or stretching out their hip joints with loud exercising music. In another corner is loud karaoke singing. T tells me the old men are checking out the ladies with a go-between, and also playing illegal *mahjong* and arranging appointments.

Near the top of the hill as the sun rises, we can see the cordillera emerge, sharp and clear as a crocodile black against the sky, from one horizon to the other, and gradually bright green patches of vegetation appear like vertical meadows on the sharp slopes.

Letters from Wales

Sam Adams

My old running mate Tom Prichard ('T. Jeffery Llewelyn' as he styled himself) had a thing or two to say about the English in Wales when, having more or less abandoned the stage, he started out as writer. In his picaresque novel *Twm Shon Catty* (1839), he writes of landowner Squire Graspacre, 'a plain, blunt, sensible man... [who while]... entertaining a most exalted opinion of English superiority... found many things in this nation of mountaineers highly worthy of imitation among his more civilised countrymen'. Gentle satire. What follows is altogether different: 'Unlike any of the half-bred English gentlemen who literally infest Wales, and become nuisances and living grievances to the people – building their pretensions to superiority and fashion on a sneering self-sufficiency, and scorn of customs and peculiarities merely because they are Welsh'. Thankfully some were different, not least among these William Coxe and Richard Colt Hoare.

Soon after our return to Wales in 1966, albeit somewhat further east and south of where we started from, I heard about 'Coxe's Monmouthshire' – a useful introduction, I was told, to the history of our new home in Caerleon. It wasn't that I ignored the advice, but other considerations got in the way. So barely a month has passed since I at last acquired a copy of *An Historical Tour in Monmouthshire* by William Coxe, 1801. Two volumes, leather-bound, 'aeg' as antiquarian book catalogues say, with hardly a scuff and richly illustrated, it is in remarkably good condition for its age. I would wager it has spent far more time decking a shelf than in the hands of eager readers.

Coxe (1747–1828) was born in London, son of a physician to the royal household, and educated at Eton and Cambridge. He entered the church, but not to stay, becoming tutor, in quick succession, to the sons of the Duke of Marlborough and the Earl of Pembroke, scion of the Montgomeryshire Herbert family. For Coxe, this deviation from his calling did not impede preferment to the Wiltshire rectories of Bemerton (a name that reverberates in literary annals) and nearby Fovant, both in the gift of the earls of Pembroke, and only two miles from Wilton House, the magnificent home of the Herberts since the days of Henry VIII. Appointment as archdeacon of Wiltshire followed in 1804. Ecclesiastical duties did not curtail a taste for travel, first indulged with the youthful 11th earl, that extended over several years and resourced a series of books: on 'Swisserland' (1779), Russia (1780), Russia, Sweden and Denmark (1781), Poland, Russia, Sweden and Denmark (1784), Switzerland again (1789). The French Revolution and Napoleonic Wars put paid to continental journeys between 1789 and 1814 for all but the most intrepid or desperate, and of course the military. What was the inveterate traveller to do? Coxe, like some 1,500 known others, went to Wales, though in his case never further than the south-east corner.

On his tour Coxe was accompanied by Richard Colt Hoare (1758–1838), scion of a wealthy banking family, who in 1783 inherited the 2,600-acre Stourhead estate in Wiltshire. On the net you will find a painting of him, a diminutive figure in his vast library. As a young man, he too embarked on extensive continental tours, which he wrote up some years subsequently: to France, Italy and Switzerland, 1785-7 (*Recollections Abroad*, 1815); Sicily and Malta, 1790 (*Recollections Abroad*, 1817). He was privately educated, but that he was a considerable classicist is demonstrated by his translation of the tour through Wales of Giraldus Cambrensis, the text used in the handsome 1989 Gregynog Press reprint. Hoare's equally handsome and far weightier original two-volume publication, *The Itin-*

erary of Archbishop Baldwin Through Wales by Giraldus de Barri (1806), is impressive testimony to his devotion to his subject. That he was also an accomplished artist is manifest in the illustrations made from *in situ* drawings that grace both his own text and Coxe's. He also provides estimates of the scope of the undertaking for the traveller intent on Wales around the beginning of the nineteenth century. It is, he says, 'two hundred miles long, and one hundred broad: from north to south eight days' journey; east to west four days'. He rhapsodises historically about Caerleon: 'many vestiges of its former splendour may yet be seen. Immense palaces, ornamented with gilded roofs... a tower of prodigious size, remarkable hot baths, relics of temples... vaults and aqueducts'. He might have been a copywriter for the Wales Tourist Board, but actually he was copying his own translation of Giraldus. For further, up-to-date details he refers his readers to Coxe who, while not an inspiring writer, is an assiduous observer and recorder of the scene.

Coxe tells us that when he and Hoare visited, Caerleon had a population of 763 and boasted a tin plate works powered by a waterwheel. He mentions a dispute over the meaning of Caerleon – is it Caer-leon, 'city of the legions' or Caer-llion, 'city of the waters', 'Caer' being 'the British word for a fortified city'? Having occasionally seen the lower Usk valley between Caerleon and Newport inundated by exceptional high tides, I can vouch for the plausibility of the latter, though the former is generally favoured. While Hoare made scores of drawings to grace the forthcoming volumes, Coxe walked the walls with local guides and located the gates of the Roman fortress, marked these days by brass plaques inserted into pavements. He remarks that the 'oval concavity, measuring seventy-four yards by fifty-four and six in depth' which 'natives' call King Arthur's Round Table is actually a Roman amphitheatre, that parts of the walls of the camp still stand, and that 'great quantities of Roman bricks and hollow tiles', stamped, as an illustration shows, 'LEG II AUG', identify the occupiers as the Second Augustan Legion.

He regretted the removal (looting we would now say) of Roman artefacts, apart from a single 'intaglio in a cornelian seal... of Hercules strangling the Nemean Lion' and would have been delighted at more recent discoveries: lower courses of stone-built Roman barracks and the baths that in their plumbing had retained a little hoard of gems, similar to the one he saw, lost by over-enthusiastic Roman bathers almost two thousand years ago. Coxe died in June 1828 and, like his predecessor George Herbert ninety-five years before, was buried in the church at Bemerton; Hoare died at Stourhead in May 1838 and lies under 'a pinnacled Gothic canopy designed by John Finch the Elder' some twenty-five miles off in the churchyard of St Peter's at Stourton.

Unfinished/Ungoverned: An Introduction to V.R. 'Bunny' Lang

ROSA CAMPBELL

This is Miss Lang, Miss V.R. Lang. The Poet, or
The Poetess. Bynum, would you introduce
Someone else as, This is J.P. Hatchet
Who is a Roman Catholic? No. Then don't do
That to me again. It's not an employment,
It's a private religion. Who's that over there?

You probably haven't heard of Bunny Lang. Or, if you have, it's because you're a Frank O'Hara fan, and can recall poems dedicated to her: 'V.R. Lang', 'An 18th Century Letter', 'A Letter to Bunny'. Or perhaps the sudden shift in 'A Step Away from Them', when he pivots from the joys of cheeseburgers, Coca-Cola and hot shirtless labourers on the streets of Manhattan to the lines: 'First / Bunny died, then John Latouche / then Jackson Pollock. But is the / earth as full as life was full, of them?' To learn that someone has died before you've even been introduced properly seems unfair – to you, to them. Yet this is perhaps how most people first meet V.R. 'Bunny' Lang, who lived for a brief and extraordinary flash between 1924 and 1956, during which time she wrote, directed and starred in numerous plays, edited a literary magazine, co-founded the first 'poets' theatre' in the United States and wrote reams and reams of startling, fervent, visionary poetry. As O'Hara says – placing her on the same cultural pedestal as the musical theatre icon Latouche and arguably the most famous American painter of the twentieth century – 'life was full' of Lang. For those that knew her, she was a 'Cambridge legend of the arts', a 'formidable presence', 'a ball of fire'.

So far, though, Lang has languished in the margins of American literary history. Despite the tireless efforts of Bradley Sawyer Phillips, the Cambridge-born painter to whom she was married for the final year of her life, her work is not currently in print – and has not been since 1975, when Random House published *V.R. Lang: Poems & Plays with a Memoir by Alison Lurie*. Featuring forty-eight poems (selected and edited by Phillips, who had been working with Lang's friends and fellow writers Lawrence Osgood and Mac Hammond), alongside the scripts of her plays *Fire Exit* and *I Too Have Lived in Arcadia*, this is a book that is now hard to come by, and Lurie's introductory memoir (which takes up almost a third of the book), though full of lively anecdotes, seems to regard Lang's actual writing as second order. Heartfelt but frivolous, it reads as part-eulogy, part-gossip column, and

is often less than flattering about its subject (rather bizarrely, it opens with a description of Lang's 'firm, fair, heavy flesh'). A small *New York Times* review at the time described it as a piece 'where resentment and affection are… thoroughly mixed'. It is perhaps no wonder that Lang's poetic star twinkled out after her death. When written about at all, she has been presented as a footnote to the rise and rise of the New York School of poets, a curio, and – persistently – Frank O'Hara's 'muse'. This is often the fate of women who happen to be connected to famous male artists and writers, regardless of their own professions or talents; relegated to the status of auxiliary, passive inspiration, they freeze into silence. The muse is not a speaking role. Yet in Lang's archives, housed at the Houghton Library at Harvard, amongst the correspondence, juvenilia, diaries, legal documents, photographs, sketches and half-finished playscripts, there are hundreds of poems, almost all of which have lain dormant for seventy years. It turns out Lang had a lot to say.

Violet Ranney Lang was born in Boston on 11 May 1924, the youngest of five sisters. The Langs were a well-to-do family – old money and a good name housed in a four-storey brownstone on Bay State Road, right on the Charles River. She was a debutante who was expected to marry – like her sisters did – a respectable man of her class, and settle into the life of a socialite, wife and mother. Instead, the young woman most commonly known as 'Bunny' became a renegade writer and theatre impresario, gathering around her a litany of now-famous names, including Harold Brodkey, Donald Hall, Mary Manning Howe, Edward Gorey, John Ashbery, Alison Lurie, Joan Mitchell, Jane Freilicher, Gregory Corso, Michael Goldberg and – of course – Frank O'Hara. The version of Lang that chimes with the expectations of her background (boarding at the Hannah More Academy; summers spent at a girls' camp in New Hampshire; formal presentation to society in 1941; member of the Vincent Club, President of the Charlotte Cushman Club) seems to lie fundamentally at odds with some of the less conventional particulars of her life. During the Second World War, aged seventeen, she joined the Canadian Women's Army Corps, because the American armed forces wouldn't take under-eighteens. She attended the University of Chicago, where she was editor of the *Chicago Review*, but dropped out and returned to Boston. There she moved through a string of miscellaneous jobs, often pulled from the *Help Wanted* columns: bridal consultant at Fabian Bachrach's photography studio, cosmetics demonstrator at a department store, researcher interviewing Pontiac owners, and – most infamously – burlesque dancer at the slightly seedy Old Howard Theatre. By 1949, with her mother dead and her sisters all married, she continued to live with her father (the organist and piano teacher Malcolm Burrage Lang) in her once-grand childhood home. Here she threw parties, some 'wonderful', some 'terrible', housed her Siamese cats, and in her room on the top floor wrote and rewrote, typed and re-typed her poems and plays. As Nora Sayre – who knew Lang in the 1950s – writes, 'she became a legend... a witty outlaw whose passions overflowed the confines of New England gentility'. Lang was the fiery, frantic core of the Boston and Cambridge literary scene: a poet, a playwright, an actress, a director and, according to Susan Howe, 'a Valkyrie'. She died in 1956 of Hodgkin lymphoma; she was thirty-two.

Lang was, by all accounts, a brilliant and difficult person. Her accolades are many: 'strong, opinionated, passionate', 'a superb comedienne' and 'overwhelmingly funny, smart, ambitious'. O'Hara's friend, roommate and sometime lover Joe LeSueur met Lang for the first time as an unannounced visitor, finding her naked in the 'grimy, grayish bathtub' of their New York apartment, from which she suggested that he make them both a drink. 'I was never so quickly won over by anyone,' he writes; she was 'someone to reckon with and adore.' Yet 'formidable' is perhaps the word used most often by those who knew her. She was possessed of an 'angry loyalty to everyone she accepted for her friends and lovers', but caustic in her criticism, brutal in her reprisals; 'once when she felt that Ted Gorey had betrayed her she sent him a Christmas card so obscene, insulting, and spiteful that he would not speak to her for a year'. At one point she became the subject of a Poets Theatre working group to 'Stop Bunny', as a result of her tendency to be overbearing and drastically over budget (she showed up at the meeting and declared them all her enemies). Once – in an anecdote that seems to typify both her incredible wrath and her impetuous creativity – she printed a thousand pink labels that read MY NAME IS STANLEY AND I AM A PIG in order to seek revenge on a man she had briefly dated, who she felt had slighted her. He found them pasted all over his New York neighbourhood; in his subway station, on the door of his apartment building, in his favourite bar, the bathrooms of his Madison Avenue office. For some time afterwards, she would sporadically send him postcards, the leftover labels pasted onto them. It is perhaps no surprise to find, in the middle of her poem 'Address to the Redcoats', Paul Gauguin's maxim: *Life / Being what it is, one dreams of revenge*.

In 1946, one of the first classes of Second World War veterans descended on Cambridge to attend Harvard on the GI Bill. Among them was a young man in a Navy workshirt who would later become one of the brightest stars in the constellation known as the New York School. It would be easy to suggest that Frank O'Hara, with his current status as a cult icon of American poetry, must have been a significant influence on his now less-

er-known friend. At the time, however, O'Hara was an aspiring musician, focused on piano concertos and Elementary Harmony, while Lang was in possession of relative local fame and a much more established literary career; she had already been the editor of the *Chicago Review* and her poems had been published by *POETRY*, i.e. *The Cambridge Review* and *Folder*. Indeed, Lang's reputation clearly preceded her; seeing her for the first time at a bookstore cocktail party, O'Hara remembered that 'as if it were a movie, she was glamorous and aloof. The girl I was talking to said: "That's Bunny Lang. I'd like to give her a good slap."' They became inseparable.

It was together that Lang and O'Hara worked out how to be poets. O'Hara recalled how they 'sounded each other out for hours over beers, talking incessantly' and argued over influences: 'We both loved Rimbaud and Auden; she thought I loved Rimbaud too much, and I thought the same about Auden and her.' It was an intense and symbiotic relationship, sustained by their shared unwavering commitment to poetry and a potent sibling-like bond (a letter from Lang to O'Hara greets him as 'Brother', while another is addressed to 'Trick' and signed 'Treat'). The two poets began a routine of 'coffee talks', daily telephone calls to talk about 'everything we had thought of since we had parted the night before, including any dreams we may have had in the meantime'. At the top of the Bay State Road house, according to O'Hara's biographer, Brad Gooch, they 'sat together writing joke poems, collaborating on alternate lines, or correcting each other's work so that it was difficult to tell whose was whose'. Indeed, Lang's poem 'To Frank's Guardian Angel' was mistakenly included in the first edition of O'Hara's *Collected Poems*, after being found by Kenneth Koch, Bill Berkson and other friends tasked with collating his poems after he died in 1966. Perhaps if Koch et al had seen the original title of the poem, they might not have been so sure it was O'Hara's; instead of the seemingly self-reflexive naming gesture evident elsewhere in O'Hara's work ('Some day I'll love Frank O'Hara', he writes in the poem 'Katy'), another draft of the poem sports the rather more teasing title 'To the Guardian Angel of an Aesthete Going to the Middle West to College'. Critics have occasionally used this editorial mishap to suggest that Lang, therefore, must necessarily have been influenced by, and sound like, O'Hara. It is too easy a rebuttal to suggest that O'Hara perhaps sounds like Lang, so instead I will turn to Bill Corbett, who claimed that the renowned New York School poet Bernadette Mayer's response to reading Lang's work was 'I like her poems better than O'Hara's'.

It wasn't just Lang and O'Hara, however. Robert Bly, another Harvard student at the time, described a coterie made up of 'an astonishing collection of intense maniacs', often crowded into a booth at Cronin's bar, with Lang holding court as 'the Circe of that circle'. This group included Lyon Phelps, George Montgomery, Hugh Amory, Sarah Braveman, Hal Fondren, Lawrence Osgood and – later – Gregory Corso, who would go on to be a major poet of the Beat Generation. Lang had met him penniless in New York and brought him back to Cambridge, insisting that he be moved into Peter Sourian's room in Harvard's Eliot House and given a job sweeping the newly-established Poets Theatre. It was this theatre that formed the hub of the New England literary scene at mid-century. In 1950, together with Mary Manning (Molly) Howe (mother of the poets Fanny and Susan Howe), Thornton Wilder and Lyon Phelps, Lang co-founded the theatre, with the support and blessing of the town's poetic grandees, Richard Eberhart, John Ciardi and Richard Wilbur. An experiment in medium, form and organisation, the Poets Theatre was to become a significant testing ground for young writers, actors, artists and designers, prefiguring the Artists' Theatre, set up in 1953 in New York by John Bernard Myers and Herbert Machiz (who would, in 1954, stage Lang's *Fire Exit*), and the New York Poets Theatre, which was founded in 1961 by a group of poets including Amiri Baraka (then LeRoi Jones) and Diane di Prima.

Originally holding the position of Secretary, and later becoming Vice-President, Lang was the only founding member of the theatre to have no formal connection to Harvard. Yet as Don Share points out, she 'was surpassed – slightly – in her publishing record only by the senior members of the theatre, Richard Wilbur, John Ciardi, and Richard Eberhart'. All of the theatre's early productions featured Lang as writer, director, actor, or occasionally all three. The Poets Theatre was more than a workshop for writers trying their hand at verse drama; it saw itself as the vanguard of an innovation in American literature. It was also a crucible for gossip, feuds and vendettas – both artistic and personal. It was DIY, underground, and often broke – no thanks to Lang, who had been known to run up colossal debts for her productions. Shows could involve Victorian gothic sets by Edward Gorey and strange costumes hand-dyed by Lang in her basement, while actors bickered over the casting of roles; it had an air of 'intentional delinquency'. Yet it also had lofty ambitions that were realised with surprising frequency: original works by Samuel Beckett, Cid Corman and Ted Hughes were staged there; it hosted the first American reading by Dylan Thomas of *Under Milk Wood*; and the first reading of Djuna Barnes's play *The Antiphon* took place in Lang's sister-in-law's Berkeley Street mansion, attended by Robert Lowell, Elizabeth Hardwick, Edwin Muir, I.A. Richards and – somewhat astonishingly – T.S. Eliot, whom Lang, never one to be overawed, had personally invited. Yet Nora Sayre remembers that 'above all, the company had an exciting aura of a counterculture, which was very hard to locate in the Fifties'.

Echoes of the Poets Theatre – and poetic drama more generally – can be seen throughout Lang's poetry, in poems composed as dialogues, in the shifts between personae and in a penchant for declarative grandstanding. In line with the group's commitment to experimentation, her writing moves between tight lines and traditional conceit to eruptions of fragmentary, impressionistic, semi-surrealist modernity. If there is a prevailing principle for the choices in the forthcoming *Selected Poems*, it has been the revelation of the immense range of Lang's work. By experiencing her work as an oeuvre – albeit a necessarily incomplete one – I hope the true breadth of Lang's accomplishment becomes apparent. She is as good at pith as she is at pathos, as skilled a

formalist as she is an experimentalist. In this, she perhaps does take after Auden, her greatest poetic love, matching his ability to shift from dramatic monologue to light verse to prose poem without sacrificing an integral voice. Often, Lang's vicissitudes appear in a single poem; she loves to undercut, to pull the rug out from under us, to begin a poem with what appears to be wide-eyed candour, only to end it with withering irony. It is perhaps no surprise that she is reported to have 'nettled' John Ashbery by telling him he took art too seriously.

The experience of reading Lang's poems is often one of astonishment, whether from the cumulative experience of the breadth of her vision or the eye-watering acidity of a single phrase. Her endings, in particular, have a tendency to knock the wind out of a reader. Part of this general air of surprise stems from the way her poetry resists categorisation. Like many twentieth-century women, she has been occasionally and half-heartedly co-opted into some of the major movements of the time. And is there something Beat-esque about her jazz-influenced interjections, run-on pronouncements and vague air of mysticism? Can we locate a New York School insouciance or urban pastoral vision? Yes! Lang *could* be seen as a stone in the architecture of these towering avant-gardes, or indeed as part of an overlooked generation of mid-century women poets, or as the rightful heir to Wallace Stevens and W.H. Auden (though the latter outlived her, in the end). But really she is a kind of singularity: more interested in archaism than Ginsberg or Corso, angrier and more melodramatic than Ashbery or O'Hara, funnier than Laura Riding, stranger in phrase and image than Rosalie Moore, and possessed of a rawness difficult to locate in Auden or Stevens. Throughout, her poetry eludes a definable aesthetic, and instead returns and returns to a state of perversity and defiance.

Such brass-necked writing could be seen to have a certain class inflection – the same entitlement that enabled her to be 'constantly praising or criticizing everyone's poems' and to be given, for *Fire Exit*, 'a budget larger than that of any previous production, yet which Bunny considered to be an insult' – giving rise to a poetic voice that feels dauntless and assured. This voice is truculent, unyielding, occasionally pugnacious, but often deliciously, viciously funny. It would be too easy to tie anecdotes such as the one about Stanley and the pig labels to poems in which rage and revenge seem to take centre-stage, yet such poems often also match the ludicrous extravagance of such a prank in their subversive playfulness, their refusal to indulge in misery. Lang also has a pastoral mode that swings between the darkly surreal and the idyllic and arcadian. Nature, for Lang, is often secretive and mysterious, enfolding itself around humanity, grasping.

On a rare hot day on the east coast of Scotland, I had my own mysterious meeting of the human and natural. Printouts of Lang's poems were strewn all over the floor – perhaps mimicking the stacks of 'papers, papers' and 'unmailed letters' that populate the poems themselves – and I was ordering and re-ordering, second-guessing, wondering what she would want. Suddenly, through the open window and straight to the top of a bookcase, flew a small bird, who sat, chirruping and reshuffling his feathers. 'He isn't a bird like the birds I've known,' writes Lang in one of her poems, 'And I've been places, and I've seen birds.' If her poems are anything to go by, she's right: birds appear throughout, from 'municipal swans' in the Public Gardens to sparrows being fed watermelon, to the 'disinterested nearness' of a pigeon. They are the prey of cats and they burst from closets, they are vocal, shrieking or singing or in some kind of conversation with the poet. They can be augurs of calamity or personally threatening. Most ubiquitous is the recurrent enigma of the white crow, which Lang returns to over multiple poems. The bird that visited me was not a white crow, but something small and brown and friendly. I didn't have any watermelon on hand, and in the end, it too flew away.

Some of the many things I have regrettably had to leave out of the *Selected Poems* are the fragments that litter the files of Lang's archive. They are handwritten in pencil on little blue sheets and scribbled in the margins of theatre programmes, typed on the torn-off top of a letter draft or hovering uncertainly at the bottom of the manuscript of a poem. Sometimes these are lines that will later be found, properly aligned in the middle of a page, a poem built around them, while others hang, like visions or aphorisms, suspended without scaffolding in uncertain white space. One such fragment appears on yet another sheet of tissuey paper, sandwiched between various typed and handwritten shards of poetry and catty comments, and reads:

Let the unfinished masterpieces hang over your life
Like a creeping shadow, let the waiting silence
Steal all of your pains and your patience

Except that 'unfinished' is handwritten in pencil over the top of a crossed-out word. In the Houghton Library, I hold the page up to the sunlight spilling in from Harvard Yard, and make out that the original word was 'ungoverned'. There is something unbearably poignant about these lines, which are impossible to read now without thinking of the truncated life of their author – meteoric in its truest sense, burning painfully bright, and flaming out. Her ambitions not fully realised and her star only half-risen, Bunny Lang had unfinished business.

Yet what is most interesting in these lines is actually precisely that shift from 'ungoverned' to 'unfinished', an edit that suggests a kind of equivalence between these two concepts. In Lang's mind, perhaps, to be ungoverned *is* to be unfinished – to write unfinished work is to refuse governance. For me, these are not lines of resignation, but of defiance. If a sense of unfinishedness permeates Lang's legacy, it is not just because of the tragedy of her early death, but also that her poems

engage with a sense of deliberate incompletion, unafraid to allow for hazy imagery, disjointed syntax, wavering speakers and frequent interruptions. In 'Poems to Preserve the Years at Home', her magnum opus, she writes, '*Not to finish* becomes the challenge', a sentiment particularly apt for a poem that seems to be unbounded by time (undefined 'Years' in an undefined 'Home') or by length, its collage of sections spooling out with the promise of perpetuity. This is a poem of inconstancy and inconclusiveness: 'Everything begun. Nothing ever finished. / Heaps and piles of waste'. These 'heaps and piles of waste' seem to mirror the poem itself, the 'boxes, papers, papers, drawers / Files... filing cabinets... especial drawers' of poems pulled together to 'preserve' a life. Anxiety about mortality permeates the sequence, as 'Time grows thin', but it is not a fear of leaving things incomplete. Instead, a fierce commitment to ongoingness is the real driving force. For Lang, unfinishedness constitutes a form of refusal, so that '*Not to finish*' suggests not only an acceptance of incoherence and incompletion, but also a defiance of endings that echoes the other disobediences and subversions of expectation seen in both her work and life.

It is that slippage between *unfinished* and *ungoverned* that I have tried to channel in making a selection of Lang's work. This may or may not have resulted in the right editorial choices, but I am less interested in presenting a definitive version of Lang's poetry than in revivifying it, opening up each poem and agitating its surface once again, after too long left in 'waiting silence'. Lang clearly wrote poems her whole life; in her archive, early works populate the pages of childhood diaries, alongside inky sketches of strange beaky figures and significant teenage plans for 'personal improvement' (apparently unrealised; she writes later, 'P.S. Violet did not improve'). Despite her lifelong devotion to writing, however, the body of work presented in *The Miraculous Season* is really a kind of flash, spanning less than fifteen years even at its outer edges, the greatest part of it written between 1948 and 1956.

In 2009, the Brooklyn-based artist Spencer Finch (another bird!) created an installation of 366 paraffin candles, arranged in a spiral on a gallery floor. Every day for a year, a new candle was lit and burned down, spreading coloured wax into its neighbour. The piece was a visual representation of 1892, Emily Dickinson's *annus mirabilis* – miraculous year – in which she wrote 366 poems in 365 days. In the poem that opens this selection and gives its title to the *Selected Poems*, Lang writes not of a miraculous year but 'the miraculous season', through which one might attempt to 'pass unharmed'. This is perhaps how we can best view her writing life; an all-too-brief spell of extraordinary time, incandescent with candlelight. On the centenary of her birth, strike a match.

Twelve Poems

V.R. 'BUNNY' LANG

Poem ('If you passed unharmed through the miraculous season')

If you passed unharmed through the miraculous season,
What now when the year runs out with chattering of teeth?
The embroidery unfinished, the pile of unmailed letters,
The echo in the empty well, what can they tell you?

The spider in the grate, the empty, indifferent weather
May be a clue. But better not to know.

The Recidivists

My first is to my finger
As my third is to my thumb.

We came in by the fire escape,
But we'll leave by the last room.

We'll take the silver and the bedding.
We're very taking persons.

Be too taken, we'll take too
The hope from your sleeping face.

Frightened   crows
Take fear and run. Their wings

Mudspattered and thin.
Rats run while you can.

We'll take you.   Take two.
Break you, break you, and as we do

We eat ourselves up with appetite.
I hate you, I hate you,

One to the other whispers.
Listen.

You are a liar,
And your cat has no gums.

I do not know the rain from the rats,
Or the rats from my thumb,

But you are a liar,
My first was the first of the world.

Poem ('You kill me')

You kill me. Yes you do.
I know no one else who'd
Buy a sparrow (I
Didn't even know they *sold* sparrows)
Just to feed it watermelon
And in public, too.

Every afternoon I think of you
Out there, flushed and fair
Scraping the exhausted rind with a spoon.
Every day! All winter.

Poem ('Then all the listening cries of nature')

Then all the listening cries of nature cry out Danger:
Sorrow my listening stick, my severage, my savage answer,
Sorrow my text and my animal bruised wonder, sorrow whitely

In the plains where the weather went to walk alone for always
I followed dumb and insolent to all the signs of stature,
Then heard the cries of nature crying Danger, Danger

The world behind me never lost without me, memory
The soft black hang – the birds that broke about me,
Burst from the closet door when last I opened it

The queer cry just distant, the crazed remembered wind,
The terminal scream of the marsh
The net like a bell that swung for us

Now heard against the fading voices, all the sprawl of dark
When animal life vanished, plants dried up and dusted down
Leaving the weather to walk alone and always, walk the stretch of plains

To Frank's Guardian Angel

*(To the Guardian Angel of an Aesthete Going to the
Middle West to College)*

May he, secure
In peacock fur
And Manner
Go in your favor,
May he wear
One crocodile tear
Stitched to the cheek at
The corner of the lid

> *You pray for him, you weep instead,*
> *Keep his appointments, bless his apartment*

Protect him from
Violation:
Bogs not creep,
Bugs not come,
Burrs not crawl
Crows fly white,
Caves not cackle not beckon;
Let him keep his Three Noses

> *Save him from the malevolent eyes of*
> *Spiders but neither throw him to the swans*

And shine on his spotted tail!
Yes on his spotted tail,
Respect his reason,
Protect his tongue

> *And in the jasmine and buttercup*
> *Season of parricide, flower him*

Poem ('Why else do you have an English Horn')

Why else do you have an English Horn if not
To blow it so I'll know to let you in.
It could be anyone, unless you do. I could be
Holding in my hand an effervescent
Preparation for the teeth, or doing swimming
Exercises on the rug, or wrapped in one,
Staring privately out the window.
⠀⠀⠀⠀⠀And I dread bagsnatchers.
Someone could be there, who would snatch my savings,
My blue glass swan I had even before I married you
All filled with quarters. Well, I can tell you,
That would be the end of our roulette games.
Therefore, use the horn, I'll never be alarmed,
I'll come at once and sing my friendly answer,
From Thaïs, you know the one, and you'll be reassured
It's me and we will both rejoice it is
The other. That is the song for which Walter Damrosch
Found so many friends in radio audiences, it goes,
WE ARE FAT GIRLS AND BOYS! WE ARE FAT GIRLS
⠀⠀⠀AND BOYS!
Then let not the others, delivery boys, Nosey Parkers,
Burglars, bagsnatchers or Red Feather representatives
⠀⠀⠀be jealous:
When you find your own true love, you will live in a house,
You too will have to have a password.

Poem ('I think I die within the year')

I think I die within the year, acknowledge
All the chaste formalities of suicide.
You'll go nowhere as you were, and if you did
You'd stand by even water shot with hatred
Having come there yourself the same.
You have to turn
Become quite simply something other than you were
So looking back to where you were, shall you say
This was not me, is nothing of identity

With what I am, with what I will be
Permit yourself this solstice, permit deliverance
A little death by skinning, stepping free
Taut skin into white skin by, the total anger
Into recommitment, honor it by ritual:
Fast thirty days. On the thirtieth day
Drink only water. Wear only secret clothing.
Speak to no one. Proceed out by moonlight only

Poem ('White of eye, blond of bone')

White of eye, blond of bone,
The victim always hunts alone:

Yes, I wore this very dress
The night that Virgil died –
And you, as stricken as you were
Remember! I believe you are
What I've been looking for,
And will pretend you were
Not married, nor had a Russian analyst,
Did not eat soup at dinner or refuse
Alcohols, or chew coffee spoons,
Or belch. Such is my faith. For yours:

I only ask you break with me
Almonds; my eyes are limes,
Now yours to squeeze. Or slice
For lemonades. My fingernails
Were not what you observed,
But dames. Not damson plums.
Not dredged with septic stains.
Ladies, ladies' hands. See, lines of pain
Perform upon the potted palms.

Poem ('I waited all that time for a bird I wanted')

I waited all that time for a bird I wanted.
In a bucket of limestone. Taking form
Like a diamond only a little more lively
The zone was horror. I stayed within the bounds.
It took place like five hundred centuries
Barely heaving. Shifting into folds and faults –
Zones and vaults. *It will come*, I said,
My strength locked up in order to endure
So that I spoke in frozen sounds, barely a whisper
It will come from that slight overture now
Overhead apparent in the mine
Wounds of the deep dead: do not bleed,
Crack and flake, shrink down
Early Monday morning we arise without echo
I learned something, though. *There is no end to the week.*
Sunday you can call it but it does not mean
That Sunday anything will end, No indeed.
Time isn't anything. It's rubbing the flat of your fist
Over a wet painting, so time comes on. Then art students
Drew little figures over it in a different medium
So time comes on, the lines imposed
On the earlier smear. I remember Elmer
In his Bathtub Period floated the ground
And put the figures on with it still wet enough to run.
You have to be terribly strong-willed to do that with time.
It's easier to go about it on a dry ground. This is all like
Found Art. VERY INTERESTING is what you say about
    effects like this.
Within the metaphor so very well might say the
    psychiatrist
Listening to this imposition of order. Very interesting.
But what are all those gummy greens, what lines
    disappeared
In the muddied colors, what oh what indeed, I know
    something else.
You never really find out. A whole new set
Of figures gets set down. You can't go back that far,
You have to find out from the future. In that future
You happen all over without end
And its smear again no line drawings. What would it be
Without line drawings. I can tell you. Terrible.

The Bear

For all I have to thank a lot I have
To thank THE BEAR. I think a lot of him,
I think of his dear ways and his unselfishness,
His merry gaze and his ingenious remarks
Which so enlivened our Saturday night card parties.
How he twinkled when he awarded the prizes for Hearts!
I remember his rapt paws caught in the first instance,
And the big teeth that sparkled when he talked to lawyers.
His undercoating looked vulnerable, somehow,
I used to watch it getting into taxis with a pang,
Or his gambols! Such savagery, into the wind,
But he was never cold, he said. I miss him!
I miss him! I shall never be over missing him.

Poem ('This time, what are the conditions of cowardice?')

This time, what are the conditions of cowardice?
A stranger bathing in the sea survived a snail...
Through all these multifarious generations I have had one idea
I have had it sick or well.

                Let the snail say now what he can,
The sun leaves the beach like the tide itself, the playing waters
Soda bright and mineral. Hitches to the sticking sand grass
Stroking the dunes. I lay away all day. A burnt match
Six feet away at my cold feet my eyes feasted bodily

Time and enough to write YOU when the weather gets holy
Reports from the sacristy now conflict with the open press
Journalists are to be seen knitting their eyebrows
                into sweaters for park benches
Seen in the park: only shoes, shoes for as far as the eye can trust itself
Time enough for comprisals when the weather is fair
And the lily light splashes out a monument from the mouths of horses
In equestrian statues. The spring makes bad.

                Out of what fen did your mother come, little
                bark-the-shin, was she competent, like you?

Subject Properties

GEOGRAPHY Very good. Enthusiastic grasp of geographical facts.
from my Third Grade Report 1932

Miss Budlong didn't know, but I
Had learned already (to my surprise)
To organize into a feeling order
The monstrosities – I was in love.
My arms ached when I watched him,
At noontime, he was taken
With the others to learn Writing –
We, the girls, learned Manuscript Printing
(Why, I've always wondered, don't
Girls have to write?) and I missed him,
My first generic memory – the unmentionable Garden.
I knew the word for this,
The pain all over, the tension
Watching, the waiting. The firecracker spontaneous
Feelings that pounced and sparked
And that unmindful little boy,
Carefully built, quietly colored,
Graceful – undertaking nothing
He couldn't conquer, like the Writing,
I used to see his arm practicing the curves
Deliberate and unhurried at his desk.
Registered already and on record
The elegance somehow of his resort.
Struck me very strongly,
I tripped and stumbled –
He went his way unhurried
Inhabiting an entirely different world.
There, that is theirs, this mine –
I was hung for explanations,
Nothing hitherto made sense
And here somehow I entered on them,
There is a difference.
What is mine is not yours,
What is yours not necessarily
Theirs. My tears were a relief.
The impossible countries, being
Indicated separate, receded
Into ordered terrains,
Flour and water.
We made relief maps, in the 3rd grade,
That year, I stopped saying the Lord's Prayer
In morning meeting. I waited
For the bolt – it never came.
Having the unanswerable answer,
I asked my mother what proof
She had in God. I got some
Silly answer – (We want to) – I felt sorry for her.

I thought. Up and through 4th grade.
At which time I discovered there were
Others who had thought the same –
That deepened my grasp of distance,
That was almost too much. But James
(his name) by his disinterested existence
Absorbed the phylogenetic consolence.
I love you so much. Don't look
When I am looking. Keep your distance.
It explains everything. I love you so much,
We speak out loud and others look.
If we spill – if we splash out –
With love, they are embarrassed.

How could I pray, I had no elbows
How could I look, without knees
Anyway, whose disorderly imprecision
Was this? Did I ask for it?
This trunk, these hands, this face?
Don't do that with your face,
Do you know what could happen, it could freeze
And you'd always look like that. I got sent
Out of class one day. I stood making faces
In the hall. The worst happened. You,
The life center, the focus of all these
Explosive abstractions, came up from downstairs
With a message for Miss Budlong. It was
All right – you smiled discreetly,
Looked the other way and passed along,
It was all right, I learned right then
To be simply embarrassed. Not the all
But only the some. But how do parents
Teach their children that kind of
Pleasant detachment? Europe, January, Mars –
The longest rivers, the highest mountains –
Altitude, Soundings, concomitant lives –
All theirs. I recognised them
But with a growing sense of
Terror and weakness, marvellous James
With nothing on his face but purpose
And sometimes, ownership.
January, Betelgeuse –
Brazil, tundra, stars,
I love you very much,
I recognise my loss
I love you very much,
I love you very much.

The Drunken Boat

NED DENNY

(after Rimbaud)

Descending the swift, imperturbable flood,
I could no longer feel the pilot's reins;
Exultant redskins had shed his blood,
Nailed his naked limbs to a brilliant stake.

I cared nothing for the fate of my crew,
Minds filled with English lace and Flemish wheat.
When all that din had been tomahawked too
The rivers let me travel as I pleased.

Into the frenzy of the tides, last winter,
As gravely intent as a playing boy,
I sped! The unmoored, errant peninsulas
Had never seen such tumultuous joy!

Tempests anointed my wakening head.
I danced on the waves, as light as a cork
(The waves, singers say, that cradle the dead)
With no tears for the witless gleam of port.

Green water seeped into my shell of pine,
More sweet than the flesh of stolen fruit.
I was cleansed of vomit and human wines.
Away both my rudder and anchor flew...

And now I bathed in the sea's immense poem,
Devourer of emerald heights, instilled with stars,
Where – obscenely pale, ecstatic flotsam –
A pensive corpse will sometimes pass,

Where, suddenly staining the bluenesses,
Slow shuddering under day's gleam-flecked tent,
Stronger than drink, vaster than music is,
The bitter reds of raving love ferment.

I've known currents, seen lightning craze the skies,
Waterspouts and undertow; I've known evening,
Seen dawns like legions of doves arise;
I have seen what man has dreamed of seeing!

I've seen the low sun, streaked with mystic dread,
Illuminate clots of violet haze,
And venetian waves flicker far ahead
With the grace of figures in antique plays!

I have beheld green nights of dazzling snows,
Slow kisses born in the glances of seas,
The pathways of strange saps no mortal knows,
Phosphorescence's blue-gold melodies!

I have followed, for months on end, the death-
Dealing rollers, stampeding the reefs,
And never believed that their haggard breath
Might be gentled by Mary's pellucid feet!

I've touched indescribable flowering shores,
Have seen panthers in the skins of men,
Troops of glaucous steeds on the far seafloor
And the sunken rainbows harnessing them.

I have watched the steam on an endless marsh,
Whole monsters rotting in the reeds and mud,
Seen water shatter in the midst of calms
And horizons stream into murky gulfs.

Glaciers and silver suns, coal-fire skies,
Waves of pearl! Grim wrecks on rusted coasts where
Giant snakes were eaten alive by lice,
Slipping from bent trees in black-scented air.

I'd have liked to show them to children, those
Gold minnows that sang in the clear blue wave!
At times I was winged by a nameless breeze.
Flower-foam grew on my wandering grave.

Sometimes, a martyr weary of zone and pole,
The sea whose sobs made my undulate way
Raised the jaundiced blooms of deep Sheol.
I knelt like a woman then, knelt to pray.

Almost an island, I rocked on my sides
The racket and squalor of blonde-eyed gulls;
Still I voyaged, while through my trailing lines
Drowned sailors sank down to sleep, gazing up...

Now, launched into birdless ether by storms
Or caught in the dank tresses of a cove,
Little boat lost whose water-drunken corpse
Neither navy nor merchant fleet could save;

Who rose out of purplish mists, smoking, free,
To pierce the reddening dome of the skies
Shot through with azure snot and solar algae,
A jam true poets taste with their eyes;

Who, stamped with the mark of electric moons,
Mad plank, black seahorses shadowing me,
Raced when the hammer of midsummer noons
Beat blue heaven into one huge chimney;

Who trembled, sensing, at vast distances,
Behemoths rutting, stupendous whirlpools...
Eternal spinner of sapphire stillness,
I longed for old Europe's time-honoured walls!

I've passed archipelagos of stars, and
Isles with fervent nights like wide-open doors –
Is it there you wait, numberless as sand,
Our promised potencies, O golden swarms?

And yet, I have cried too much. Dawn haunts me.
The sun is grievous and the moon is foul.
My timbers are warped with love's lethargy.
Let this keel splinter, allow me to drown!

If I think of a shore in Europe, it is
The black pool in twilight's fragrant grey
Where a child, bowed with sorrow, releases
A boat frail as a butterfly of May.

I cannot, drenched in the opiate tides,
Float once more in a cotton ship's wake,
Or endure the great flags' and pennants' pride,
Or suffer the prison hulk's terrible gaze.

An Asterisk on the Map

SINÉAD MORRISSEY

This is the text of a keynote lecture that Sinéad Morrissey delivered at the Ciaran Carson Conference, held at the Seamus Heaney Centre in Belfast on 14 September 2023

Ciaran Carson's *The Star Factory,* first published in 1997, a year before The Good Friday Agreement, offers, in his own phrase, an 'alternative hologram' of Belfast, pieced together by memory. All memoir is pieced together by memory. The term *memoir* describes its provenance as a genre. *The Star Factory* is striking, however, in drawing our attention to the maverick ways in which memory actually works, to Ciaran's laterally associative leaps and flights of cognitive fancy (I will return to flying soon), and to his submission to serendipity as the book's organising principle. 'Everything you open seethes with memory', he writes, describing, with his hallmark lavish attention, the contents of his writing desk drawer, which he has, just now, opened, prompted to do so, of course, by thinking about something else:

Let us concentrate, instead, on the contents of a drawer filled with bits of string, a bunched red fist of rubber gloves, empty cotton reels, an elastic-bound, dog-eared deck of cards, a two-point electric plug, a measuring tape, two brass door-knobs, three mouth organs, and a solitary knitting-needle – these are but some of the objects I retrieved just now, perusing one adjacent drawer of the table under the machine on which I'm typing. How many hands of cards were dealt? How many conformations? How many skirts were hemmed, how many buttonholes? What wild tunes were played? How many dirges? What squeaking cleanliness of dinner plates? How long is a piece of string?

'Let us concentrate, instead'. 'Following my non-linear dictates'. 'Rambling ambiguity'. 'As I beat about the bush of this book'. 'Which brings me back'. 'Which puts me in mind'. Through the interlocking mechanism of such right-angled conjunctions, one senses the sleight-of-hand of a narrative running away with itself, *à la* Laurence Sterne's *Tristram Shandy*. One also senses, rightly, that Ciaran could, at any juncture, have written brilliantly about anything.

Memory isn't linear, like plot, or the time continuum, but rather disembodied and free. It disrupts the normal rules of the universe. Accordingly, *The Star Factory* does not provide the reader with a conventional beginning, middle and end. It is not chronological. Very little happens. 'It has been suggested that the mind of the storyteller is inhabited by constellations of... crucial points, whose stars are transformed or regurgitated into patters of the everyday', Ciaran points out, ten pages before the opening of the above drawer. Which tells us, explicitly, that the narrative shape of *The Star Factory* is, itself, star-shaped – pointy and dazzling at once. That, like light beams, the musing loops of the book extend from and return to a single radiating point: a derelict shirt factory on the Donegall Road. That the 'asterisk on the map' of Ciaran's most famous poem, 'Belfast Confetti', is turned inside-out in *The Star Factory,* so that the map is an asterisk, too.

From the outset, this derelict shirt factory is introduced to us as totemic, atomically unstable; as symbolically more than itself:

The Star Factory has long since been demolished, but bits of its structure still lay at the back of my mind. Floating through its corridors, ascending its resounding Piranesi iron staircases, or wading through a flooded loading bay, I realised that for some time I had confused the Factory with other establishments, or other purposes, and its dimensions had expanded.

Taking my cue from this abandoned star factory whose 'dimensions have expanded', which Ciaran places at the centre of everything he wants to say, I place at the centre of everything I want to say today his book of the same name. Upon its spiky triangulations and star-points, I hang my personal tribute. Taking my cue, equally, from Ciaran's own 'non-linear dictates', his sideways jumps and disjunctions, I bump from one subject to the next. I have no great insight to offer, either on Ciaran's work, or on Ciaran himself, but envisage what follows as a form of *correspondence* – one of Ciaran's favourite words – part homage, part parallel, part answering-back-after-the-fact, like a letter his beloved postman father might have delivered to a house whose occupant has already left, leaving no forwarding address.

The doppelgänger, the fetch, the uncanny lookalike, whose life mostly mirrors one's own, is a figure Ciaran thought a great deal about. 'Sometimes, with a doppelgänger jolt,' he writes, 'I recognise this is the real world, only slightly altered from when I last visited, or was invited, and I acknowledge my shadow.' Though they never, as far as I'm aware, actually coincided, one of Ciaran's presumably multiple fetches, or shadows, was my father – their lives proceeding along eerily adjacent lines to such an extent that my relationship with Ciaran was imbued with the unsettling sense that we'd already met before we met.

Born on 9 October 1948, two years and six months after my father, who was born on 22 April 1946, the two boys grew up on literally parallel streets, my father at 80 Sultan Street, Ciaran at 100 Raglan Street, separated only by Balkan Street and Plevna Street, in that corner of the Lower Falls in West Belfast named, in the call-and-response manner of Empire, after the Crimea. Undoubtedly Ciaran and my father would have crossed paths dozens of times, even if they didn't know it.

Both Ciaran and my father were fundamentally connected to the Nationalist Catholic culture into which they were born, yet tangentially separate to it in usual ways: Ciaran because his family was Irish-speaking (unusual in the 1950s; the language has gained greater ground since); my father because his family was Republican, then later Communist. Both Ciaran and my father had charismatic, famous-in-their-own-right fathers of their own: Ciaran's father an Esperantist, storyteller and Irish speaker extraordinaire, who appeared on BBC Radio Ulster's Irish-Language *Desert Island Discs,* choosing 'the language itself as [his] sanctuary'; my father's father a larger-than-life radical activist, ex-IRA internee, Honoured Guest of the Soviet Union (twice) and May-Day Marcher extraordinaire. Both of these fathers brought both of their boys up the same 'broken limestone, cold-stream pouring pathway from the Whiterock

Road' to walk along the top of Black Mountain towards Hatchet Field, Ciaran's father regaling his son with tall tales in a language I do not understand; my father's father regaling his son with different types of tales – the Battle of Stalingrad, the Long March – which also turned out to be species of myth, though my five-year-old father didn't appreciate this at the time.

Because Ciaran's father named one of his sons for his brother, Pat, there are two Pats in *The Star Factory*: Ciaran's brother, whom he calls on throughout the writing of the book to fact-check; and his uncle Pat, who was interned during the Second World War as a member of the IRA. My father's father named his son for his brother, too, so that in my father's family there was both a dead Michael Morrissey and a living one. My grandfather, also, was interned during the Second World War as a suspected IRA terrorist, also with Ciaran's uncle Pat. If Ciaran and my father never consciously met, Ciaran's uncle and my grandfather undoubtedly did, on Strangford Lough's prison ship the *Al Rawdah,* or later in Crumlin Road Gaol. 'I was locked up with the best and brightest of my generation', attested my grandfather of his internment years (1940–5). Born into poverty in 1921 in the Markets area of Belfast, the year the map of Ireland was torn in two, my grandfather could never have dreamed of staying in school past thirteen, never mind of university.

Which – as Ciaran himself might have said – *puts me in mind* of the NI Education Act of 1947, also mentioned in *The Star Factory,* and which 'guaranteed free secondary education for all denominations'. In Ciaran's formulation, the 1947 Education Act was held by some a catalyst 'for the onset of the current Troubles, as the educated Catholic students of the '60s took to the streets to demand Civil Rights for all, and we all know what happened after that'. The direct beneficiaries of this Act, both Ciaran and my father not only attended secondary school until the age of eighteen, but university for free, with generous maintenance grants to boot. In my father's case, he did, as Ciaran here predicts, march around Northern Ireland demanding Civil Rights for all. In Ciaran's case, *The New Estate, The Irish for No, Belfast Confetti, First Language, Opera Et Cetera*, et cetera, et cetera, are precisely what happened after that, and the rest, as they say, is history.

*

I first encountered Ciaran on television. I was in Dublin, in the second or third year of my degree at Trinity, in my friend Síle's parents' living room, and a man with a dense moustache and intense demeanour was reciting a poem directly at the camera. He had a Belfast accent. Though we'd missed the beginning because we were all talking, whatever the man was saying soon grabbed our attention and we turned our heads collectively to watch him. The poem was 'Belfast Confetti'.

The way this man was reading his poem felt like a kind of measured assault, each word born far off at the back of his throat, precisely angled through the human machinery of articulation – uvula, tongue, teeth, lips – and shot out into the world. The poem wasn't so much describing an event (a riot in my home city, something which, in my eighteen years living there, I had never personally witnessed) as becoming the event it described. 'Belfast Confetti' was a happening in its own right.

'Who was that?' I asked the room, once Ciaran had finished, and the programme had moved on to something else.

'A poet from the North', said Síle's mother, stating the obvious. Nobody in Dublin seemed interested in the North in 1992. The North, or *The Black North*, as some of my friends called it, who had never actually been there, might as well have been the moon.

But I was transfixed.

*

'Or, according to another narrative', continues Ciaran:

the Factory contained a great secret. Beneath the ankle-deep oily water that covered the terrazzo floor of one particularly murky corridor, discarded or lost objects could be detected shimmering: keys, watches, gold rings, a salamander broach, fountain pens, the porcelain arm of a doll, like things scattered on the sea-bed from some titanic wreck.

As soon as he introduces it, the Star Factory transmogrifies into something else. A shrine for votive offerings. The site of augury. 'They called this the Zone', he says.

Though Ciaran and I sometimes talked about films, and about Werner Herzog in particular, we never spoke of Andrei Tarkovsky's 1979 masterpiece *Stalker*. Either Ciaran had watched *Stalker* before writing *The Star Factory*, or the Star Factory, in the writing of it, took on the mysterious powers he describes. In *Stalker*, unhappy, philosophical individuals – it's the 1970s in the Soviet Union, unhappy, philosophical individuals are ten a penny – pay a kind of dark-tourism tour guide to take them into the Zone. A former site of heavy industry, the Zone has since become wilderness, through which the three protagonists make their way towards a room in an abandoned factory where their secret wish will be granted. Here, just as Ciaran describes above, beautiful black fish swim in shimmering pools above objects tossed, or lost, or left behind: a hypodermic, an uncoiled spring, a hubcap, a dish, a ladle, coins, tiles, pottery shards, an icon of Christ the Redeemer.

Like Tarkovsky's *Stalker*, the book *The Star Factory* is a paean to vanished manufacture, conceived, as Ciaran writes the 1916 Easter Rising was conceived, in quasi-liturgical terms. 'The air was full of grit and glitter', he says, remembering a demolished railway station from the Age of Steam. Glassworks, ropeworks, foundries all make an appearance. 'Unbearably tall mill chimneys teetered against the Atlantic-grey sky, churning out thick ropes of smoke like fleets of armed destroyers.' Black smoke billowing from factories, thickening the atmosphere, is a *leitmotif* of the book, linked, synaptically, to the smoky interior of churches, with their candlelight and rising incense – twin escape routes to heaven for wandering souls. When Ciaran stumbles into St Mary's on Chapel Lane after a session in Kelly's Cellars in order to experience the hallucinogenic trip of a Tridentine

Midnight Mass, the Star Factory, because it is never far from anywhere, is waiting for him there. 'Here', confesses Ciaran, 'dazed by chanted Latin, incense, alcohol, and candlelight, I find myself an eight-year old clothed by the Star Factory, barely kept from sleep by the coldness of my crisp, snowy, cotton Christmas shirt.'

As a boy, then, Ciaran was clothed in relative luxury, instilling a love of sartorial elegance that stayed with him for the rest of his life, and in marked contrast to earlier generations of Belfast children who, he reminds us, were dressed by their mill-worker mothers in flour bags. Like strange angels, these women haunt the pages of *The Star Factory*, women Ciaran precisely describes as 'that army of female linen workers – doffers, weavers, winders, tenters, rovers, spinners, drawers, peelers' – trust Ciaran to know all their proper names – 'who occupied the Lower Falls'. I don't know if Ciaran's mother was among them or not. He barely mentions her in his book. But my father's mother was, and this description of her compatriots reminds me of the day I asked my grandmother about her job in Conway Mill when my father had been a child. In a rare instance of intimacy, she'd proudly retrieved her set of precious wooden tools left over from her factory-floor days, one of which was carved like a mushroom, and let me hold them.

*

'The Underworld reflects the world above, seen through a glass darkly', affirms Ciaran of Jean Cocteau's movie *Orphée*. As though I've fallen into the same film set, the boyhood living room Ciaran describes in *The Star Factory* is a replica of my grandparents' living room: the same open coal fire its focus ('did you know focus in Latin means hearth?' Ciaran once asked me); the same knick-knacks on the mantel; most weirdly, the same pale brown ceramic brooding chicken, guarding its clutch of ceramic eggs; the same sofa. On this very sofa, Ciaran, as part of a crew of three or four children, 'flew to Turkey and back in the space of a day':

We would always remember the sherbet fountains, the elaborate hubble-bubble pipes and refractory camels, the scent of kif and kumquats drowsing through the alleyways and cool arcades; when night came, as suddenly as brushed mascara, we knew it was time to leave.

Shortly after beginning his tenure as Director of the Seamus Heaney Centre, wearing, if I remember correctly, the silk paisley-patterned scarf he'd bought with his Forward Prize prize-money in 2003, Ciaran asked me for a lift home one evening after an event in the small back common room. I was driving a ramshackle fifteen-year-old red Ford Fiesta I'd bought for £200. For some reason I *can't* remember, the back seats were down and both the back and boot were filled with a large wooden door. Medbh McGuckian had already bagsied the front passenger seat.

'I'm so sorry Ciaran', I said. 'But I don't have room in my car.'

'Why not?'

'I've got a door in it.'

'A door? Show me', Ciaran said.

And so I'd led him to where my car was parked outside. The wooden door crammed into the back of the little car was massive.

'Sure I can still get in there', Ciaran insisted. 'I'll lie on top of it.'

'But what about a seat belt?' I asked.

He didn't deem this worthy of a reply.

I opened the boot.

With his remarkable skinny agility, Ciaran climbed inside, pulling his knees in behind him, and lay on the door facing the ceiling, like a mummy in a sarcophagus preparing to negotiate the tricky passage to the afterlife. I drove carefully, shepherding the two poets who lived five minutes away from each other in my own childhood stomping ground of North Belfast home. Occasionally, Ciaran would flip over to point out a necessary lane-change. He was clearly enjoying himself – getting a lift home on a door was second-nature to the man who'd flown to Istanbul and back on a sofa.

Getting a lift home on a door was also second-nature to a man who could grow and shrink at will, for in *The Star Factory,* Ciaran's frequent teleportations to alternative universes often involve abrupt changes in physical size. Just as he likes to 'float', 'hover', and above all 'fly', he especially likes to shrink – the act of suddenly growing smaller granting him access to hitherto inaccessible spaces. Of the family 1950s radio, he writes:

I would press my ear against the big warm humming Bakelite body, and mentally shrink myself to walk about inside its Toltec labyrinth of valves and tubes and crystals, sometimes encountering giant dust-beetles who would scan me momentarily with alien antennae, and then go about their scarab business of managing the dark interior.

Worlds within worlds, effortlessly conjured and explored. In *The Star Factory,* given reality is friable and paper-thin, prone to dislocation, peppered with worm-holes and portals, into which Ciaran swiftly disappears, fulfilling a secret wish which both terrifies and inspires him in equal measure: 'to be invisible'.

*

Whether walking, floating, or flying, or simply reinventing himself from book to book, consumed by new enthusiasms, Ciaran was always travelling. On a few occasions I had the good fortune to travel with him, to Boston, Aldeburgh, Washington, Paris. In Paris we visited Notre Dame. It was Lent. The statues were covered in shiny purple cloth. 'It's because they're really alive', Ciaran explained. In Boston, at the annual AWP conference, Ciaran took one look at the thousands of American students and professors of Creative Writing pouring over the shopping mall concourse bridge into some vast anonymous conference centre and promptly turned the other way. 'So many', he said, quoting Eliot, quoting Dante. 'So many. I had not thought death had undone so many.'

But I liked randomly coinciding with Ciaran best. By chance. By serendipity. In *The Star Factory,* Ciaran writes of serendipity (perhaps his all-time favourite idea):

I confess I never knew the derivation of this word, until I looked it up, just now, serendipitously, in Chambers Dictionary. Serendipity, the faculty of making happy chance finds.

If we just happened to bump into each other, with no preparation or pre-set protocol for interaction, I was more likely to catch Ciaran musing, or more accurately obsessing, on whatever was currently preoccupying him. Ciaran had the fiercest attention of anyone I've ever met. One afternoon, we bumped into each other in the upstairs concourse of Belfast Central Station, which I believe has since, like so many Belfast streets in Ciaran's poems, changed its name. Not having yet read *The Star Factory,* I was unaware at the time of the pleasure Ciaran took in railway stations, or, more accurately, in the entangled network of railway lines extending out from a central point – another asterisk, in fact – which formed yet another alternative map of the city in his consciousness:

The whole elaborate system of junctions, sidings, and crossovers is corroborated by interlinks of rods and levers, wires plumbed into black tubing running parallel to the track, under intervallic staves of telegraph wires strung out between high poles, as the sleepers below exude oil and creosote, and the heraldic armature of railway signals click their intermittent semaphores, trying to orchestrate the movements.

Ciaran asked me when my train was – I think he was en route to Dublin, and I was heading home to Whiteabbey – and, given we both had half an hour or so, suggested a coffee. He was wearing a hat. He took it off and placed it carefully on the seat beside him before turning to his black espresso.

'Do you know the man responsible for doing away with hats?' he asked.

'JFK?'

'Exactly.'

Then, *à propos* of nothing:

'I'm reading Paul Celan.'

I didn't know very much about Paul Celan. Mortifyingly, I'd once played audio of Paul Celan reading 'Death is a Master from Germany', in German, with no translation, to a group of stranded English Literature sixth-formers in the Peter Froggatt Centre at Queen's in a misguided attempt to convey something about rhythm. But there my knowledge of Paul Celan more or less ran out.

'Do you know what Celan is really all about?' asked Ciaran.

This time, I didn't know the answer.

I shook my head and waited.

'The *sentence*', said Ciaran emphatically. 'What's a sentence? What's a preposition? What's a conjunction? *And*?

'*But?*' '*However?*' 'After each conjunction, where does the sentence travel?'

A fusillade of question-marks.

'With Celan, you might think you know where you're going in a sentence one instant,' Ciaran continued, 'but the next instant you discover you don't.'

He sat back and put his hat on.

'Right', he said, checking his watch. 'Bye.'

And was gone.

I felt I'd been gifted something.

On another occasion, he called into my office upstairs in the Seamus Heaney Centre. On my whiteboard on the wall, I had a list of titles for poems I hadn't yet managed to write. One of these titles instantly caught Ciaran's eye.

'The Millihelen', he said. He didn't ask me what it meant.

A couple of days later, he caught up with me in the corridor.

'Sinéad. The Millihelen. I looked it up. *That's a very good word*', he said.

I felt pleased to have introduced Ciaran Carson to a word, rather than the other way round.

'Did you know it isn't in the dictionary?' he added.

I did not.

'And by the way' – he was amused – 'you spelled it wrong.'

*

When I left Belfast in early summer 2017, I didn't manage to say goodbye to Ciaran. He wasn't feeling very well at the time. But he called round to my friend Emma's house with a box for me. The box was hard-edged and white and smaller than a shoe box. It was patterned with blue ink spots, running slightly, blurring around their edges. Inside: two black-and-white postcards of Belfast City Hall, tram-lines criss-crossing in front of it. A second-hand Croxley fountain pen from 1940 in its own yellow and black cardboard receptacle with the words *A Dickenson Product Made in Great Britain* printed on the side. A bottle of indigo Quink ink. A rectangular blue-and-white striped cloth. Two matchbox-size adverts for Gallagher's cigarettes. A colour postcard of *Fish Magic* by Paul Klee. And two tiny ivory Japanese *netsuke* drummers, one facing his drum, one looking my way, dressed in kimonos, holes for dressing cords drilled neatly into their backs.

Ciaran and I began a correspondence in pen and ink, beginning with a thank you letter from me for such exquisite, careful presents, using the Croxley fountain pen. 'I'm glad the pen suits your hand', Ciaran replied, in exquisite fountain-pen ink of his own. In May 2019, after his terminal diagnosis of lung cancer, I came over to visit Ciaran and his wife Deirdre, when he was writing his final masterpiece-collection, *Still Life*.

After I got back, I sent him a letter on several postcards I'd picked up randomly from a storeroom at work in Newcastle University, designed by Tara Bergin's husband. Ciaran wrote back (this time by email – time was running out):

'Thank you for your little cornucopia of cards. I was pleasantly startled to find the name of Antonio da Messina on the first of your cards (The Poet as a Child). It was as if you'd been reading my mind! – the same painter nearly made it into my Yves Klein poem. See attached draft. Did I mention the name to you, or is this just pure serendipity?'

*

Another idea which increasingly fascinated Ciaran was the *Aisling*. In an *Aisling* experience, the poet falls asleep and sees a vision, and in this vision a woman – traditionally the spirit of Ireland – demands to know of the poet what he's doing for her. Ciaran came to see all poems as forms of *Aisling*: acts of translation from the dream world to the written world, their inspiration, or source, mysterious, given or withheld at will. Like his father before him, Ciaran's sanctuary was language itself. 'I, too, hide in language,' he writes in *The Star Factory*; 'in this respect, at least, I am my father's ilk.' 'It's not about you,' he'd reiterate to his students, exasperated by undergraduates because they'd never heard of Kafka, 'it's about the language.'

If I first saw Ciaran on television, I saw him last after he'd died. Perhaps he'd become his own *Aisling*. It was January 2021 – the beginning of the second UK national Covid lockdown. I was having a difficult time and no one in my family could come over to help me. One night, though I wasn't sleeping very well, I fell asleep and had a dream. I was sitting on a bench on Royal Avenue, outside Castle Court, watching the river of shoppers flow past, when I spotted Ciaran walking towards me. He was wearing a hat and a coat that must have cost around £500. He had a handkerchief in his top breast pocket. He sat down beside me and talked. When I woke up, I couldn't remember what he'd said – the words themselves had evaporated – but they'd been funny, bright, enthusiastic; mercifully impersonal. I felt as though he'd visited me.

'Driving on the M1 at night south of Milltown', writes Ciaran in *The Star Factory,* of Milltown Cemetery on the Falls Road:

you can observe a curious optical phenomenon, as the headlights of the passing traffic bounce off the gravestones and the black stone eyes of archangels in an orchestra of random constellated Morse, like the flash outburst of Olympian photography in colossal stadiums, and you feel the dead are signalling to you.

For Love by Robert Creeley[1]

JAMES CAMPBELL

On a small, handwritten poster affixed to a noticeboard in one of the university's communal spaces, I read the words: 'Robert Creeley: A talk'. Date and time were given, as well as a room number in one of the eighteenth-century buildings in Buccleuch Place which housed English faculty seminar rooms. The speaker was announced as Will Robbins, not a name familiar to me.

In the autumn of 1977 I was entering the final part of a four-year English degree course. During the academic session to come, as in the one lately ended, I would be pursuing my chosen specialization, American Literature. Many such talks took place on campus. Anyone could give one and anyone could attend. Just organize the use of a room, usually at lunchtime or after classes at 5.30, advertise your subject, and... talk. 'Michael Boyd will speak on Ben Johnson's "Sejanus". All welcome.' That was one I attended. A prominent figure around the university as a student, Boyd later became the artistic director of the Royal Shakespeare Company. At a more official level, Quentin Bell and John Wain entertained us with accounts of, among other things, Bell's biography of his aunt, Virginia Woolf, and Wain's book about Samuel Johnson, just published. A youthful Roger Scruton lectured a small group on aesthetics, not neglecting to toss disobliging references in the direction of the architecture all around, including the building in which we were assembled. Saul Bellow, in town to receive a prize in the name of the Highland novelist Neil Gunn, of whom he had until then lived in ignorance, took questions from the American Literature students in a room high up in the same building, the David Hume Tower, answering their earnest inquiries with smirking replies. And now Will Robbins, whoever he was, would talk about Robert Creeley.

I was surprised to come across the poster. The Black Mountain poets, of which Creeley was the most prominent member, formed a marginal grouping, but modern American poetry was made up of such groups, and the Black Mountaineers – as they were sometimes referred to, not without a hint of disdain – were the most mainstream of the marginals. Since my Glasgow days, I had been attracted by their linguistic adventurism and variety of content and form, even by their obscurity. None among the main figures bore any resemblance to the others. Charles Olson had the status of a priestly figure; Robert Duncan had links to a separate group, loosely known as the San Francisco poets, but was happy to profit from the amplification offered by the Black Mountain brand; Edward Dorn, originally a student at the college that gave the poets their team name, had become a personage in his own right with the cult success of his long poem *Gunslinger*. Over the course of the 1960s, Creeley's renown had outstripped that of Olson, making him the central player. Where they were fashionable at all, it was mostly in youthful literary circles of an outsiderish taste.

In terms of poetic-political affiliation, Creeley was practically an American literary neo-nationalist, claiming association to William Carlos Williams on the one side, the Beat writers on the other, with Walt Whitman guarding the rear. Both wings were subversive, being essentially anti-Eliotic, setting up a resistance to the anglophilia conjured by that name. My taste, to the extent that I could make a claim on such refinement, was in a constant state of becoming. My interest in the Beats was largely restricted to the deranged genius of William Burroughs. At the time, I probably hadn't even read Ginsberg's 'Howl', and certainly not *On the Road*.

For Creeley, however, I had something like a post-adolescent crush: his cool manner; his references in interviews to jazz and painting, with claims that Miles Davis and Jackson Pollock were influences on his practice as strong as that of any writer. Lines from the Creeley pen were gestures, emotional as much as aesthetic, like urgent strokes on an action painter's canvas, or the fluid line of a phrase by Miles, improvised according to the mood of the instant. American voice was the heart and lungs of the practice. 'I begin where I can, and end when I see the whole thing returning', he wrote in one of the pithy notes he appended to his books. His collapsed left eye was sometimes covered by a black patch, the other eye supporting a broad, agreeable face.

I followed Creeley's syncopated prose with fascination in a book of pieces called *A Quick Graph*, and in my jejune efforts at writing criticism tried to catch its tone. Most of Creeley's essays were scarcely identifiable with literary criticism. His sentences stammered, went back on themselves, qualified their own statements, resisted qualifications – 'so to speak', 'as it were'. His short stories, collected in *The Gold Diggers*, were likewise mannered. Imitation of Creeley's poetic action, most frequently characterised as 'nervous shudders', was a well-advertised trap, though that did not prevent me from falling into it.

I memorised the date and time of the talk, and knew I would be there.

Going by appearance alone, Will Robbins turned out to be a surprise proponent of the work of a writer like Creeley. My mental snapshot is of tweed jacket, open-necked button-down shirt, trim chinos (though we had yet to learn the word) instead of blue jeans or colourful cotton flares or whatever rumpled garb we turned out in. He looked about thirty and spoke with a well-bred American accent.

1 from *A Philosophy of the Literary World in 20 Book Titles*

I sat amid a group of fifteen or twenty people. Nothing of what he said remains in memory, only a broad picture of a man – clean-shaven, neat hair, not tall – standing at a lectern. What came out of the event, mainly, was a feeling that here was someone with whom I could assuage my loneliness, a literary loneliness. Few people I knew on campus were committed to literature in the way I felt myself to be. It was another world; it held out the promise of consolation, the way religion does for some. It demanded the worship not of one God but of many, and the dutiful study of texts. It asked for faith, though mystery remained, for in numerous cases neither diligence nor subservience would result in understanding. It was as if a treasured novel (*The Sound and the Fury*), a set of poems (Creeley's own) or a collection of essays – James Baldwin's, for example – offered guides to conduct, with hidden keys to a richer life, in the sense in which 'richer' matters most.

I read and re-read my authors – those three not least among them – with an instinctive hunger that gripped and steered me in other essential areas: the pursuit of love, the soul's connections, the body's carnal recognitions – so deep in the bone, so unpredictable, so demanding of satiety – being the obvious ones.

When the speaker concluded his talk and shuffled his papers, I approached. He had that easy-to-like American manner I was familiar with, and without awkwardness we arranged to meet. We began to take lunch together in the Men's Union dining room, a late-Victorian site of old-world throwbacks, middle-aged waitresses dressed in shiny black costume with white satin piping, the more elderly among them addressing their young charges as 'sir', the others as 'dear' or 'love'. We arranged to play squash in the well-appointed sports facilities on The Pleasance, named presumably for its prospect of the great mass of Arthur's Seat, positioned as one guardian of the city to the east, balanced by Edinburgh Castle to the west.

At the lunch table, or in the café after the game, which Will usually won, he and I discussed not only books and writers but also magazines of different kinds, another subject of close interest to me. It wasn't clear why he was in Edinburgh. He was finishing off an advanced degree of some kind, with a medieval focus. His interest in the Black Mountain writers was not as intense as mine. In fact, his proper studies were at an extreme divergence. This did not strike me as unusual: people read Chaucer on Monday and Pound on Tuesday; Pope in the morning, Lowell in the afternoon. It emerged that Creeley was or had been a teacher of Latin. I found this an appealing item of background knowledge. It thickened the texture. It was even more surprising to learn that the avant-garde poet with the piratical eye-patch had once bred chickens for a living, exhibiting them at fairs and coveting prestigious rosettes.

Will's background and present life were anything but marginal. He came from a middle-class family in the state of North Carolina. His father was employed as some kind of advanced engineer on the space programme NASA. For the time being, Will lived with his American wife in the picturesque village of West Linton in the Pentland Hills, a short drive from the southernmost suburban fringe of Edinburgh. He owned a car, a rare possession even among post-graduate students, in

which he travelled to and from the campus each day. He spoke of his devotion to the *Times Literary Supplement*, then at its intellectual peak under the stewardship of John Gross. Select members of our own English faculty were published in its hallowed columns, including the eminent professors, Alastair Fowler and Wallace ('W. W.') Robson.

Will read the *TLS* diligently, as he did the avowedly left-wing *New Statesman*. Both of us treasured the *Statesman*'s chic books pages, but I recall Will's scornful opinion of the weekly parliamentary columnist, James Fenton, then emerging from his public-school Trotskyism. Will disliked the way Fenton habitually resorted to personal abuse, not stopping short of mocking politicians' facial features, bodily tics, hairstyles and other easy targets.

I enjoyed my conversations with Will, as I always did with someone of superior intellectual authority. The impression made on me by his intelligence was that it mirrored his style of dress: compact and proper. He was sympathetic towards me, a touch paternal, which I didn't mind. He asked about my intentions after the completion of my present course, as people did, an inquiry to which I could find no satisfactory reply. I had dreams – as yet they could not be labelled ambitions or even hopes – of working for one of the weeklies, such as those he and I read assiduously. But those magazines were based in faraway London, peopled by the Fentons, the Christopher Hitchenses, the Martin Amises, the Julian Barneses, to cite only those within reasonable casting distance of my own age. They were comfortably of the world of letters, already engaged in writing the next chapters of literary history. I was a so-called mature student of dubious qualification in Scotland – the provinces, in their eyes – with an eight-year gap in formal education at my back. In time I would understand that the gap formed an integral part of my education, but that time had not yet arrived.

There was little to complain of. I enjoyed my studies, and the company of a few friends, among whom I could now count Will Robbins. We spoke of the novels of William Faulkner, in which I immersed myself at a level of intensity inspired by no other author. Will said that, as a white Southerner, he and his kind lived their daily lives under the weight of a heavy ancestral moral burden, made of past and present wrongs. Much of the Faulkner corpus was rooted in this uncorrectable history, which contributed to the extraordinary character of both its baroque content and ultra-modernist form. I was endeavouring to correct the wrongs Will referred to in my own way – not didactically, not even deliberately, though not entirely without awareness – by being engaged with the writings and public attitudes of James Baldwin, and, contingent on that devotion, with the work of other black writers, some of which formed a part of our enlightened American Literature course.

Early in the New Year, Will invited me to spend Friday evening with him and his wife at their cottage in West Linton, where I would stay overnight. I accepted gladly. I looked forward to it as a break in the routine of Saturday morning visits to the library, attempts at a story or poem (I had just about exorcised the nervous curse of

Creeley), the yawning gulf of weekends, long city walks, sometimes extending as far as the Pentland Hills. On Friday evenings, solitary pub visits with a compact Baldwin or Mailer paperback for company, three or even four pubs on the itinerary, a pint to drink and an essay to read in each, salt-and-vinegar fish supper in the interval, eaten the proper way – with fingers – while walking from one pub to the next, or loitering in the street.

On a winter evening, once university activity was over for the week, Will and I met at the Meadows end of Buccleuch Place and drove out of the city towards the Pentlands, he with the latest *TLS* safely folded into his solid leather briefcase. He told me that normally he would read it from cover to cover over Friday evening and Saturday morning. This weekend would be an exception. His wife had prepared something appetising for dinner. We would drink wine, gossip about the English tutors and discuss politics, mostly American.

Rosemary Robbins turned out to be exceedingly pleasant. Her complexion and all-round good nature matched her name, a warming blend of herb and songbird. Her eyes, set in a rounded face topped by fair hair tied back, were shining and happy. She and Will conversed in a manner that gave off the radiance of contentment.

At the dinner table, the question of my future plans naturally arose. In Will's view, there could be nothing better than to apply to pursue post-graduate studies at Oxford or Cambridge. Those towering universities occupied the academic summit in his eyes. The possibility of such an elevation seemed unlikely to me, though I had pondered the chances of remaining at Edinburgh, studying for some vague qualification under one of those sets of initials that other people seemed to deal in without self-consciousness, writing critical papers for scholarly journals – on what? Creeley? Faulkner? Baldwin? Or Robert Duncan, about to be the subject of my final-year dissertation. I might end by drifting into teaching without really ever having intended to. As a career, it wasn't my first choice. I had in truth no plausible choices. My hopes of making my way in the literary world, by one route or other, offered no discernible set of directions to follow. They were only hopes – half-hopes – not plans. Before the time of my final exams, I would come to a decision and would make my commitment, but I did not know that yet. And Will, without his ever being aware of it, would have a role to play in my resolution.

When dinner in the cosy kitchen-living room was over, we set about clearing up and washing the dishes. Here the men came into their own. Will, now in unbuttoned humour, three or four glasses of white wine to the good, wiped the soapy cloth across each plate in turn, rinsed, then handed it to me for drying, chatting all the while, at one minute directly to me, at the next to Rosemary, who was seated by the fire, about me. His manner had a noticeable but inoffensive element of condescension. We got on well enough. Why else, after all, would I be there? Rosemary's quasi-maternal presence added something to the atmosphere that I liked. I enjoyed the dual consciousness of being here, at home in rural Scotland, albeit not my native corner, in the midst of their cultured, prosperous Americanness. Among the exotic domestic practices I observed was the habit of keeping large quantities of coffee beans in frozen storage. The essential place that coffee occupied in daily life – its quality, its density, its origins, all topics of serious discussion – was a surprise in itself.

Rosemary announced that her unmissable Friday evening habit was to listen to Alistair Cooke's *Letter from America* at 8.45 pm on Radio 4. I occasionally listened to it too, in my Edinburgh flat, and was happy to join in. Did Will put his *TLS* aside on other Fridays to sit with his lovely wife by the fireside, both enjoying the veteran English journalist's charming, mid-Atlantic recitation of yet another moral tale drawn from his deep cracker barrel?

Now we settled together, the radio tuned to receive the BBC through the frosty Midlothian air. Over dinner, Rosemary had talked of politics, mentioning with visible pleasure her father's approbation of Adlai Stevenson – the ideal candidate, he believed, for a twentieth-century president. Americans, as I already knew, talked of presidents past, present and future – about politics generally – with an assumption that non-Americans in the company knew exactly who they were talking about, what the policies were, which characteristics were to their advantage, the reasons for approval and disapproval.

No British person would have spoken instinctively to outsiders about Labour or Conservative party politicians the way Americans did about their leaders. They were figures of global importance. Americans respected our parliament and perhaps our monarchy, at the pinnacle of our system of government yet invested with no significant power. They spoke of those institutions with the respect properly paid to ancient establishments and quaint traditions, but most Americans back home wouldn't know even the name of our prime minister, far less any members of the cabinet. We, on the other hand, tossed around the words Nixon, McCarthy, 'the Kennedys', Kissinger, as if they were characters in a play in which we ourselves were actors. Our play was lacking in drama. Theirs suffered from too much of it: Vietnam, Cuban Missile Crisis, Cold War, racial segregation, riots and assassinations, Kent State.

The admiration Rosemary's father had for Stevenson had been passed on to her, and it was evident as she spoke of one man that she looked up equally to the other. Stevenson, I discovered later, had stood for president twice in the 1950s and had been defeated on both occasions. At the time, I had never heard of him.

Only night was visible against the cottage windows. Only Alistair Cooke's voice was audible, harmonised by a chuckle or murmur of assent from one or other of my hosts. His suavity warmed our cocoon.

We were interrupted by a knock at the front door. It came without warning. Any sound of approaching footsteps must have been overwhelmed by the radio. Rosemary and Will exchanged questioning looks. A neighbour? There were few neighbours in the vicinity. The house was on the remote side of whatever notional boundaries the village looked to.

Will disappeared into the hall and opened the front door without first asking 'Who's there?' This was West Linton, not South Side, Chicago. A muffled American voice rolled down the hall, more affirmative than Will's, authoritative and deferential at the same time. Stepping into the living room, the visitor brought the cold air in with him. Tall and broad-shouldered, sporting what suddenly appeared as a very American crew cut, he greeted Rosemary with brisk courtesy. 'Mrs Robbins.'

Already on her feet, she welcomed the newcomer, with whom she was obviously familiar. He had arrived by car and hadn't troubled to pull something warm over his shirt. I was presented as a friend of Will's from the university, information that prompted reflexive politeness. Conscious of disrupting an intimate gathering, he wished to be to the point in whatever he said or was said to him, though it wasn't clear to me, and evidently not to Will and Rosemary, what the point would be. He was – I can't be sure he used the expression, but something like it – 'just checking in'. If there was nothing to report, that in itself would vindicate the effort he had taken to get here. Vague impressions made themselves felt without my taking note of them.

All four of us remained standing in the living room. Some further words passed between the newcomer and Will – inaudible to me but not uttered with caution, or as if in code – before the two men turned their backs on us and went into the hall, or perhaps another room, where more tight sentences were exchanged, hard to hear. They then returned to the living room for the brisk formalities of departure. The guest was offered something to drink, but declined. He had been with us for only a few minutes. Standing straight, he turned to Rosemary and said 'Mrs Robbins' in the same way, before nodding in my direction. Then he faced Will and saluted.

'Captain Robbins.'

Will acknowledged the salute with a facial expression of assent. He accompanied the visitor to the front door.

Back in the living room, we did our best with the stifled embarrassment. Half-explanations spilled out, and were as quickly tidied away. Will used to be in the army, Rosemary said. The visitor was an old acquaintance, stationed somewhere nearby. I took those remarks at face value, still not fully aware of what had happened. Will's army career had not arisen in our conversations in the Men's Union dining room or in the café we sometimes went to after squash games, only his father's involvement in NASA. I was ingenuous but in the manner of a child, taking in more than I was capable of understanding. Some mysteries of this kind lie dormant for years. It was clearly not a subject they wished to talk more about, and the same went roughly for me. We would all happily have returned to Alistair Cooke, but the broadcast was over.

So where were we, before this started? Weren't we talking about the political leanings of my favourite English tutor, a Yorkshireman of committed left-wing views, of whom I was an eager admirer, though for his infectious literary enthusiasm and acute insight more than his politics? Yes... well... anyway... great guy.

We rounded up the evening amicably enough, and went to bed. The next afternoon, after a late breakfast and a walk along country lanes, Will accompanied me to the centre of the village, where I was able to catch a bus back to Edinburgh. Nothing more was said about the unexpected intervention of the night before. There was no immediate noticeable change in our relations. The visit had otherwise been a pleasant occasion.

A second trip to West Linton followed in March, this time without Rosemary who had flown to Pennsylvania to be with her lately widowed mother. As the academic year progressed, however, our friendship cooled. On one occasion, Will stood me up at the Pleasance squash courts. I waited half an hour, racket, shorts and post-match towel at the ready, before giving up. When accosted later for an offence I have always found hard to excuse, Will shrugged it off sulkily, saying he had pinned a note to the board that hung in the entrance to the sports centre. A note? Among fifty surrounding notes?

As the time approached at which I had to submit my dissertation to my tutor – a 12,000 word essay on an American literary figure of my choosing, to be graded as an integral part of the degree rating – Will offered to read it in advance. A leading figure on the West Coast poetry scene, Robert Duncan was as unlike Creeley as it was possible to be, though they remained allies in the campaign to liberate American poetry from Europe's tonal dominance. In the essays collected in *A Quick Graph*, Creeley repeatedly reaffirmed his devotion to Olson, Williams, Louis Zukovsky and others of similar grain. Nothing could be less like his own muted line than the ethereal unit that flowed from the mind of Duncan. His vocabulary and sometimes his spelling were ostentatiously archaic and precious, now gothic – as he might have put it, 'Gothicke' – now North Beach hip. He had written a suite of poems as variations on some Elizabethan English lyrics, published by a small publisher in Ohio. The copy I had bought at Compendium Books in North London was among my most prized possessions. Duncan could sound at times like someone who, once started talking, finds it difficult to stop. I learned later from people who knew him that this was often the case.

My tutor had advised against this choice of subject. He tried to steer me in the direction of John Berryman, author of *The Dream Songs* and a sequence of sonnets addressed to an adulterous lover. Berryman was more accessible than Duncan and, not incidentally, the object of much topical critical commentary on confessional poetry which, it was assumed, would nourish my judgements. The so-called confessional poets were in vogue: Berryman, Robert Lowell, Sylvia Plath, Anne Sexton and others.

It was their very popularity that had put me off. Something more 'outside' was what I wanted. That was my favoured association. It was less an effect of intellectual audacity than an adolescent leftover. I didn't seriously consider even Creeley as a topic, though he might have offered a more negotiable quantity. Duncan lacked Creeley's allure, but I stuck with him.

Criticism on Duncan was next to impossible to find in Britain. Even his own most recent collections were hard to come by, though the latest among them could be obtained through the inter-library loans service. I photocopied every page and stitched the loose quarto leaves together into a makeshift book before returning the real one. Some time before, Duncan had sworn off publishing for fifteen years – though not off writing – and publicly chastised his publisher, John Martin of Black Sparrow Press, for failing to structure lines on the page in the precise way in which he wished them to appear. He was the sort of cult writer of which there was no equivalent in Britain, and was not well known even in the US. Hardly anyone in the English department at Edinburgh would have been familiar with his name. Those who were would have read little, if any, of his work. Who was going to judge the quality of my dissertation?

For those reasons among others, I was pleased to have Will as a first reader. He accepted my carefully typed script one lunchtime before we headed to the Men's Union dining room, and slipped it into his leather briefcase. When finally he returned it, having kept it longer than I expected, I was dismayed to discover that he had jotted marginal comments in red ink, sometimes just asterisks and crosses, on every page, which meant I would have to type it all over again. He was not complimentary about the contents.

'Do you want me to critique this at the level of grammar?' he asked. I didn't know how to reply. I had been at Edinburgh University for almost four years, and had written a score of well-received course essays. I had recently succeeded in placing some almost Creeley-free poems in reputable Scottish magazines. An article had been published in our mutually admired *New Statesman*. No one had hinted that the work was in need of remedial treatment 'at the level of grammar'.

I declined the offer and retrieved my script.

Relations with Will had slowed considerably, though not to a total halt. About halfway through the term of our friendship, I had started seeing a young woman from Glasgow, with a Scottish mother and a Nigerian father whom she had never met. She was pretty and witty, with a characteristic Glaswegian blend of comedy and acerbity in her everyday talk, surprising at first, but all the more delightful for that. It wasn't a deep affair – she already had an attachment at home in Glasgow, about which she did not mislead me – but it was fun, and my existence was in need of some fun. She and I occasionally took lunch in the dining room, where we were served by the uniformed waitresses. Sometimes we would wave to Will, seated at another table.

One afternoon, not long after the exchange about my dissertation, Will caught sight of me in the university library in George Square and ambled over. Was I still seeing Carole? Occasionally, yes. Not as regularly as before, though I didn't feel the need to explain the ins and outs. He and I did not have that sort of friendship.

'She was in the dining room today, you know', he said. There was a pause and a smile that I disliked. 'With another guy.'

He might have thought he was merely doing his fraternal duty. As, perhaps, he had been doing his duty in inviting me to West Linton to talk about politics, with an emphasis on the leftward leanings of my tutor; in reading up on Robert Creeley and advertising a public talk, with author and location selected to attract young rebellious types. Was it legitimate to see those as being among the typical designs of an American secret services plant on campus? My wider acquaintance included some people in the university Russian department, students and teachers, who told of being contacted by MI6 and invited to an interview. It wasn't a career offer, at least

not at this stage, but there could be advantages, monetary or otherwise, in keeping half an ear cocked as fellow students moved through the corridors and put the world to rights in neighbouring pubs and cafés, passing on the occasional note, with special attention reserved for those who urged protest, confrontation, speechmaking, picketing, joining, fomenting yet more protest. No one I knew had ever taken the bait – but then, if they had I wouldn't have heard their stories.

It is possible that Will really was, as Rosemary had wished to suggest in her awkward attempt at smoothing over, a retired US Army officer. Once a captain, always a captain. But why would a former enlisted soldier be subject to unannounced visits on Friday nights in the Scottish countryside? It would be reasonable to conclude, rather, that he was an active secret service officer and a bona-fide post-graduate student at the same time. Surveillance duties in the sedate Scottish capital would have been light and occasional, mainly self-selected and running in happy parallel to his other concerns, though real enough for all that. In respect of those more-or-less improvised duties, I suppose I was his dupe, even though I think he genuinely enjoyed my company, at least at first. He tolerated it, until a note pinned to the crowded sports centre noticeboard signalled that the process of offloading had begun.

No harm was done by his remark about Carole, sly or otherwise. On the contrary, the day of 'She was in the dining room... with another guy' marked a turning point in my life. I could hardly have any objection to Carole meeting someone else. In fact, I knew the fellow she was with that lunchtime, a friendship that predated her association with me; not a boyfriend or any kind of rival, but a lively character with whom she laughed a lot. She was often laughing, and so was he: short, baby-faced, gay. She spoke of him so fondly that although we had met only once or twice, and then in passing, I felt as if I knew him.

Will's surveillance instincts were nevertheless sound, if only indirectly. I had been aware of Carole's waning interest. I had spotted her in the dining room that very day, as I approached the entrance, but had retreated and gone in search of lunch elsewhere, hoping she hadn't seen me. She had returned to the university after a recent break, having spent the holiday in the same house, the same bed, with the legitimate 'other guy' in her life – her husband. That relationship, too, fortunately childless, was waning, and would be over before our student careers came to an end, though the outcome was to be in yet another guy's favour, not mine.

It was on the same day that a promise was made between myself and me. The promise announced itself on the short stretch of road between my flat and Edinburgh Central Library, just past Greyfriars' Kirkyard. It urged me to take hold of my goal – a modest goal – to steer it by force of will, to chart a route to that realm of half-hopes, follow it at the expense of other vague objectives, and to welcome the risk of failure.

One weathery Friday afternoon on George IV Bridge.

Three Poems

JANE YEH

On Geraniums

This morning, I refilled the vase where roots were sprouting freely,
Tickling the water. The cuttings seemed like lush fingers; they wanted

To grow as far as possible. In the filtered light I wondered if my gardening
Knowledge would be sufficient for them. I thought of how, as a child, I'd

Failed to keep alive a small chameleon in a tank, its dry, delicate skin, how
Whole pieces would shed periodically like leaves (which is normal). After a while

It died for no reason. If I was merely unfortunate in this, like a Moomin
On a bender hitting a cyclist, perhaps the motor vehicle of my husbandry

Could be certified safe in the present. The other geraniums in my flat have
Peculiar forms, woody and bent like tree branches. Age makes them go wrong

(Or lack of pruning). I wasn't sure if cutting them short would actually help
Them to flower – it seemed counterintuitive, like smothering a purebred kitten

Or hiding a hot dog in someone's pocket. When I was nine, a boy I didn't know
Gave me a single carnation. I was so embarrassed that I handed it off

To a teacher. This is to say that being surprised by flowers isn't always a good
Thing (to this day, I find carnations distasteful). My geraniums originally

Produced an abundance of buds, like eager acquaintances. The drama
Of their stalks was gratifying, even though I hadn't done a thing besides water

Them regularly. Imagine being so keen to display yourself, over and over –
All that effort. I could never show so much devotion to blooming. In fact,

My interest in geraniums is a relatively recent phenomenon. To care for a living
Thing with no purpose is a luxury, like filling a whole room in your house

With tortilla chips. I'm learning to appreciate how a leaf can thrive instead
Of a flower, how it persists in growing. The patience of how it lives.

Almost Like Being in Love III

To be dunked like a lobster tail in a pool of butter.
Or enrobed in melted cheese like a fondue.
It's like sitting in a hot tub in the Alps with your friend group when a bear goes by.
The feeling of being in a movie becoming the feeling of being in a hot tub in a movie.
Like when your reflection in a mirror moves separately from you for a second!

The tap of a ball-peen hammer on a ceramic plate, like space music.
What the owners of a possibly haunted house call French doors…
It's like making netsuke out of a horse chestnut you found on the street in Barking.
What if the hammer is actually tapping on your skull?

The snap of a metal tape measure retracting, when it catches your fingers.
It's like trying to cut into a whole cheesecake with only a plastic spoon.
Or trying to brush your teeth with meat paste.
The feeling of walking into a possibly haunted house with a netsuke collection on show.

The thud of a trunk being dropped on a wooden floor.
What if you hear a door creaking open behind you… but you're in the middle of a field?
It's like viewing your body from all sides in a three-way mirror (yikes).
Or seeing a possibly haunted steak that your friends don't remember putting on the grill.

What if the trunk is actually the inside of your chest?
Like hearing a tiny bell go off when you step on a concealed metal plate.
It's like looking into a hot tub filled with spaghetti.
Or waking up in hospital scrubs in a faraway field…

What if the hot tub is filled with béarnaise sauce, not spaghetti?
What if the middle of a field is actually the inside of your skull?
What if the steak is really your heart, which has somehow been removed from your chest?
It's like waking up in a stranger's bed in a possibly haunted cupboard.

Haribo Lane

In this story, you've never been happier. The flowers are real
but look like plastic. You bring strawberry casserole to the
potluck dinner. All your neighbours like you, even though you
have the pizzazz of a carrot. Every dawn, you open the
ludicrous curtains and prepare to brandish the day like a
roasted turkey leg, sipping on a coke bottle with the furious
verve of a dehydrated camel. You're never lonely on Haribo
Lane. Like a prawn cocktail at a luncheon, you've never been
so popular. You walk to the gym for your weekly badminton
session, where your opponent, Henry, resembles a friendly
ciabatta. That night you sleep the sleep of a champion. If only
you'd moved here sooner. You feel oddly at home in this
environment, like a boiled lobster on a parsley-adorned
platter. One day you walk to the mall, where you work
designing topiary animals for window boxes. Your boss,
Sandra, resembles a frightened pincushion. When the
shadow of a ginormous fried egg looms over you, it's a wake-
up call. You always knew it. In the final scene, you speed out
of town like a banana on a moped, hugging your briefcase of
essentials to your chest with the practised death-grip of a
senior octopus. The sky is all the colours of a burger, and the
trees wave their leaves fondly as you skedaddle away.

Five Poems

HEATHER TRESELER

Sparrow

Song, for you, is mostly male,
mostly advertising. 'Ladies,

for a good nest and good time –'
In the arthritic maple and linden

trees of this tidy self-regarding
suburb, dozens of bird banjos

strum with an insistence usually
blamed on rowdy hormones.

*

I can't help but think of Catullus
in his mortgaged villa, back from

serving empire, finding little joy
in his familiar bed as he spins

in the torn sail of his sheets, pining
for Clodia, whose talent is seduction.

Whose sultry gaze and long-legged
stride inflames him while she ignores

his pleas, letting a pet sparrow tease
and sate her lust instead of his own

eager member. As if congress were
a law of perfectly mutual enactments.

*

As if the trees, warbling with urgency
and wood, pantomime the almost

alimentary need for touch – or the tragedy
of flourishing in just one settled plot.

Oh, sparrow! An ancient Roman stirs
in your feathered chest, deejays a bawdy

carpe diem, playing Darwin's bell
in the morning ballad of the hard sell.

Honey and Silk

Days of the body's ripeness when it has gone too long
   untouched, pendulous as fruit nuzzled by bees
      playing piñata with gravity, one's limbs

full of the syrup of hoarded light: I think of you, north
   of here, waking in bed without the small climate
      of my body, how you conjure the feel of naked

legs before you stir to answer the phone or call of day.
   We are both lovers and citizens of the wallet,
      and you have wanted me to have work's

rewards though it means weeks apart, shuttling back
   and forth, cold spells in a forlorn bed. I think
      of Clodia, Catullus's muse, whom Cicero

decried from the senate floor. How dare a widow,
   married *sine manu*, flaunt the freedom of her
      fat inheritance in rowdy bacchanals

with men of consequence? Senators, to whom an
   unmarried woman's chosen pleasure signals
      danger in an empire of fathers and sons,

frail fabric of patrimonium. Respectable women were
   meant to spin the family cloth and stay clothed.
      Clodia, boss of her boudoir, did neither,

donning imported silks, charming the demimonde,
   and letting Catullus churn in verses, yearning
      to hoard her decadent kisses, the thrill

of honeyed limbs. We know little beside her wealth,
   her want: Catullus's longing, Cicero's terror.
      But I think of my love – and my equal

need for freedom – and wonder if she was mistaken
   for fruit when she was a roving bee, living on
      the honey of her own manufacture, wearing

the life (and silks) that pleased her, taking a lover
   who'd also take *leave* of her, so she could wear
      the sheer bright robe of her lonesomeness.

Noli me tangere

After William Merritt Chase's 'Modern Magdalen' (1888)

In the late afternoon, we went to the museum
to amble shyly among its images, to study
a soft question curving

in a nude's spine beneath an argument for wings
in her shoulders' blades. Pinions, whiter
than sunlight on new snow,

edged in a shadow of their own making. A breast's
bare and delicate handful. The rose soles

of naked feet. In silence,

we note the supple staircase of blue-gold skin like
a monk's freshly pressed vellum –
or a voluptuary hour not yet

begun. In her hidden look, our thoughts are abreast,
abed, not admitting our want of her,
our figural third, our portraiture.

Sophia Hawthorne: En Plein Air

Ecstasy, from the Greek *to stand outside oneself*,
as the painter, gazing at her subject, slips from her body

or as in moments of extremis, great pain or pleasure –

when a door falls open
and the soul hurriedly departs.

I had always wished to leave. For years, I thought
I'd perish in my mother's house, pitied invalid, bled and leeched,
dosed with mercury and opium, case beyond all cure.

Then Hawthorne appeared in our dim parlor. My soul
met its adamant: a quartz to debride my flesh
of the tiresome troubles of family –

father, who never made enough money. My sisters, teaching school
for our rent, bread, and honey. Our hapless brothers, wont
to guzzle and gamble, flirt and cavort while mother fretted

in endless prayer,
high-minded lamentation.

How dreary – this perpetual earning
to eat and mate, mother and suffer.

I yearned to make.

So, I did: paintings, landscapes and likenesses.

Then sculptures, a bust and medallions. I trained my eye
in the alchemy of oils, my hands in clay, pining for the rigor
of quarried stone.

Already an author,
Hawthorne parsed the shadows of a saturnine home.

Like me, he abhorred the days' slop and grind, the endless commerce.
Doubtful as Thomas, he yearned to craft earthly
beauty, and he did not see me as the runt, the sickly Peabody.

But as an artist. And as a woman, no less.
To the taper of never spoken hopes, he brought flame: heat and kindling
of a man's heart, intent on its obtain.

Against the riddle of my daily pain – headaches that blotted
out sun, sound, and sense – he pledged desire, a sympathy better than
any tincture.

I studied a blush that crept across his brow in parlor trysts,
the light's skitter over the dark lakes of his eyes. At night,
I conjured his smell of ink and leather, the gentleness
with which he took my hand.

Yet we would have no marriage –
no hearth – until we found the Old Manse.

Nestled in that sunlit house by the banks of Concord River,
we strode across the broad field where men had sowed blood
with ardor for freedom, so that private wish might be

the only king.

One night, after he coaxed me to stand outside
myself, to let the last door fall open –

I took the ring he had lent my hand
and carved our names
into a window pane

with two truths: *Man's accidents are God's purposes* –
and, in an image granted to my painter's eye,

the smallest twig leans clear against the sky.

Leda

She had put on his knowledge. But he did not know
she also took her share of power – the Yeats scholar,
swanning into department meetings with his china
teacup and armorial tweed. She had first met him
at the new faculty luncheon where he waxed wise
about local real estate and research funds. Later, she
wondered: when had he planned to tell her that he
chaired the tenure committee? Before the first drink?
After he stepped, uninvited, into a kiss inside her door?
He styled himself a man of Ted Hughes intensities –
his ghosts, his crows, his horsey eyes that brimmed
with mention of Alfred Lord Tennyson. Woundedness
was his game with women like Zeus donning feather
boas, that preposterous bird suit. She knew the trade:
her acquiescence, his backing. Given the stakes, should
she take the sacking? If she declined and he retaliated,
she'd have the long fraught duty of making her case –
the grim air of jurisprudence in the HR office, some
dim thirty-year-old official unable to spell 'fellatio.'
But if she accepted one night's trespass, she could cite
the landlord's scruples and get him out before breakfast.
Clearly, he did not see she was from Sparta: a generation
of women who, as girls, watched mothers suffer –
and swore they would never pay that tax without
burning down every last priapic Troy. So when he
finished with a birdie flourish, she pet the little beak
and dry webbed feet imagining how, some years from
now, a bright axe would fall and she would baste him.

Three Poems

LUCY HOLME

Prosciutto

Phosphorescent in the pan, incongruous – like us
at our first meeting. All that thin, petty crackling –
colliding by chance in a nightclub – never wholesome,
never clean. On the sticky basement floor, rising steam,
a crush of sweat and belonging. In those days, food
was a boring distraction, at most a box to be ticked.
Before insatiety. We never cooked; I never got to see
the city through a soft-focus Ottolenghi lens, you picked
me no *fiora di zucca*. No, only microwaved lasagne
from your mother's freezer. Offered burned pancetta;
scant scraps of a richer dish that might sustain me. Soft
crumbs from a *sacripantina* was the most I could hope for,
to pick them off your sweater one by one, to know such
sweetness was transitory, and that I was not your choice.

Breaking Up in Fort Lauderdale

This strip mall has all you need in modern life – acrylic French tips and personal
injury lawyers, creams you can't get over the counter in Europe. In Walgreens
you traipse the aisles bathed in medicinal light – *Neosporin* for your paper cuts,
Benzocaine for your haemorrhoids and under-eye bags. It could be midday or
4am – that fish pill smell slaps you wide awake. This is a place you can get
organised. You can wax your bikini line and photocopy without missing a beat.
You like the low hedging in the parking lot but the spaces are too narrow for
your SUV. It took six months to get used to the South Florida grids, to the fact
that no-one walks around here. It is Friday, date night. You meet in a squat
brown room in the rear of the Benihana Buffet. The chefs throw eggs in the air
and you catch them in your water glass with a half-bow. She asks who will ever
love you like that again as you read the set menu in silence. *At least you are
married,* she says. *Isn't it a bit late to start again?* You drink your Sapporo and
nod. She thinks you should *make it work.* You look across to Bodies by Cindy,
neon buzz dissipating. It is too late, of course. All vestiges of love iconography
neatly packed away by the time you came to be here, eating hibachi shrimp
with her. So now two love stories have to end. Like a broken satellite connection,
the signal drops out, re-loads. The mailbox pings. You seek answers without
the right questions. Ask if you should dare to strive for more. But she says *no.
Don't strive, just fix it.* At that interview in Paris in the winter of 2002, you were
friends at first sight. In smart Whistles suits & low-heeled court shoes. Jet-lagged
and over-awed, you told stories while making cocktails for the boss. In the end
it was a face that fits which mattered most. Luckily they liked you both. There
are no words left to say tonight. You close the tab and pay. You will always have
teppanyaki at SE 17th street, though you never had much more besides. You
stand and hug, thank her for her advice. *You are tired of love like this.*

A Review of the Mushroom Restaurant

We drove miles in the wrong direction to Triora
to try a little place that had been recommended –
but found it had closed. The owners were too old
their health too poor and when we were redirected
to another little place that specialised in mushrooms
it was not as expected. The new restaurant served
only local *porcini* and *ovulo buono*, orange and smooth,
with the consistency of regret. We did not complain
about the lack of variety – we were, after all, unfamiliar
with the species and how they grew, we were hungry
and it was late. We didn't anticipate so many courses –
risotto, tagliatelle, gnocchi, chopped up atop *steak tartare*.
I had never thought of mushrooms as the main act,
had always put them last. As a garnish, not the prize.

That Man's Scope: Dudley Young (1941–2021)

ADRIAN MAY

1. Writer and teacher

'There's been a war between science and poetry, and poetry lost', announced the barefoot, tall, bearded man in the big lecture theatre, to a room full of nervous first-year literature undergraduates. It was one of the first few weeks of lectures at the University of Essex in October 1993, unusually still summery. The man standing by the lectern was Dudley Young, speaking without notes or a script, as was his particular custom. I later learned that he made this a point of honour.

As I mature student, my immediate thought was that he was talking my language. Dudley was already known to be somewhat controversial and unconventional, even for radical Essex. He had come to us via Canada and Cambridge, where he had been accepted for postgraduate study, after announcing that he 'wanted to lose an argument', as he told me later. Everyone had an opinion about Dudley Young.

Later that year I applied for his second-year class called 'Primitive Mythology', which I managed to join despite a long waiting list. He spent two weeks talking about the first two books of Genesis. So much from so little. He would speak for an hour, then have questions and discussion. I still have my notes. The level was higher than anything else I had experienced. Other classes were complicated and intimidating, but this was air that was exhilarating, talking of Edens, good and evil and original sin.

What strikes me now about his memorable opening words is how uncompromising they were, hinting at his radical, reactionary engagement with and critique of the whole Enlightenment project of progress and rationality. And this was on the campus that had practically invented the Enlightenment as a first-year course, still compulsory for all humanities students in those days. It was a challenge and an unusually wide statement, and too confident for the cautious world of academia. Young's writing style and teaching style, as I discovered, were the same: to many students stimulating, to others maddeningly counter to their careful considerations.

By then, I had a copy of his *Origins of the Sacred* (1991), which read, happily, like his talk, high-flown but accessible and full of memorable sentences. It had made many 'books of the year' lists in the serious newspapers and quickly gone into paperback. At one time he was offered a job at a major university in America on the strength of it, which he turned down, preferring to stay on his farm, out in Abberton, with a view of the reservoir.

His book on Yeats, *Out of Ireland* (1975), was unavailable and the university library copy had been stolen. It is worth finding, as I since have, as he is one of the few writers on the poet who takes the influence of magic seriously, putting it into context with the times and culture, as well as giving close readings of the poems themselves. Here, it is Yeats's own breadth, a quality Dudley shared, that he emphasises: 'By giving access to the past and the future, the poet can offer us some hope of access to the present'. Later in the same early section of the book: 'What gives the poet such a wide metaphoric range was that his Irish situation was analogous to that of Western Europe, about to shatter…'. He thus accepts Yeats as a 'mage/poet', a description that takes Yeats on his own terms and accommodates the seriousness of his art. Worth a reprint, surely?

Origins was altogether bigger. As John Gillies, the Shakespearean professor from the department, said at Young's funeral: 'How can a person write about all that, connecting up so many dots from such distant deeps and skies, and still be a solid academic? Such cultural breadth wrong-foots the contemporary academic mind.' So what is Dudley saying in this huge-scaled magnum opus? When I was re-reading it after his death, this paragraph, from chapter six, leapt up at me, as will happen with other sections, to anyone tuning in to it:

Thus what I am advocating is not primitivism but *neo*primitivism, a retrieval of archaic (and childlike) attitudes that takes account of intervening developments. I am not suggesting we simply jettison science and bring out the tom-tom. We must begin at the point where science obviously lets us down, in the representations of the forces that move us to dream of love and war and beauty. We may then go on to discover that pre-scientific man did it better – guided in our travels by our best poets, such as Yeats... and Stevens, who against extraordinary odds, have never lost the thread.

It seems inadequate to quote a small bit from such a big book, but reading through Dudley's contributions from back issues of *PNR* helps show his thought, as well as his humour. You can hear this in the earliest paragraph that is available online, from 1978:

The problems are formal, all right, maybe they always were. No one can wear a suit any more, and jeans get sloppy. Charles Uptight in his three-piece whatsit may pronounce with severity, but we suspect he's schizoid, left his body uptown whereas Denim Dan, in his leftover grooviness, holds his body, for sure; but he's a-syntactical and has an attention span of about four seconds.
('On Bertrand Russell's *Autobiography*')

One of the books Young talked about writing when he retired was going to be about Dionysus, of whom more in Part Two. A line from 1979, about Michael Herr's work on Vietnam, sums up his view: 'Dionysus is angry, and the price we must pay for having blasphemously suppressed the ritual discharge of our wild energies is to be overrun by them.'

There is a lyrical piece about his church (1980), which was next door to his house, where he is 'slipping into the time machine of evensong'. The long essay on twentieth-century literature, based around Orwell ('Still Life Inside the Whale') from 1981, is refreshingly unlike anything anyone would dare say now, while his memories of friendship with Robert Lowell and his time at Essex in the seventies are revealing. It is his overall freedom that we now only seem to be able to admire from a distance.

Elsewhere there is a farewell to Donald Davie, founder of Literature at Essex, presumably when he left, and a long excerpt, again from *Origins*, where another bit leaps out and links thematically with the quotation above: 'If we are to repair what one might call the "narrative dislocations" in our scientific culture, we must put ourselves back to school with our forebears, to recall the myths that legitimise our existence and tell us how to live with godly power.'

Raymond Tallis's review of *Origins*, from 1994, emphasises the 'awe inspiring erudition' which is also 'not difficult to read' and is a good introduction to the scope of the book, from a scientist and poet. To paraphrase G.K. Chesterton – and you could talk about people like him with Dudley – myth sees the bigger picture, while we remain clogged in detail, and this seems even truer in the age of the internet. With his writing, you feel able 'to see all ages in a sort of splendid foreshortening', as Chesterton said in the 'Prefatory Note' to *The Ballad of the White Horse* (1911).

Later, when I knew Dudley, I could sense in him someone who suffered from his refusal to compromise. He once expressed disapproval of creative writing as a subject and I remember us having a mock wrestling match as we argued. His point was that the mysteries of creativity should remain taboo. 'Your effing book is as creative a book as I've read', I told him as we struggled in the departmental corridor, while nervous academics were already peeping with prurient curiosity from their quarter-opened doors.

He was proud, so he kept quiet about his near misses with fame. It was only recently that I learned that a TV company was going to film him teaching for a series, but somehow the director got fired. He was interviewed about Robert Lowell, who had stayed with him at Essex. Dudley is quoted at length in Ian Hamilton's *Robert Lowell: A Biography* (1984), and a section of Roger Deakin's *Waterlog* (1999) is devoted to him. He wrote for the *New York Times Book Review*, the *LRB* and *PN Review*, and was a personal friend of Donald Davie. There is a plan to hold something like a symposium on *Origins* at the University of Essex.

When Dudley retired I regularly invited him into my classes to talk about mythology or about Yeats. When he came in, he would talk for two hours about two short poems, 'The Second Coming' and 'Leda and the Swan'. In my 'Writing Magic' class, he said a very memorable thing to my writing students: 'your job is to turn dream into prophecy'.

Dudley's writing and teaching were as one. His Primitive Mythology class would have made a book and I am glad I still have my notes. He once pointed out that the two most influential people in Western civilisation, Jesus and Socrates, never themselves wrote anything. Yeah, and they were *teachers*, I could have added.

I had dedicated my own first book to Dudley and to my old friend, the poet Robert Hill, as 'my myth teachers'. These two never met but they died on two successive days in 2021. The funeral for Dudley took place in the church beside his farm. I read a poem by Yeats, 'The Fisherman'; while John Gillies talked about *Origins*, Richard Gray read a Wallace Stevens poem and Herbie Butterfield a section from Thoreau's *Walden*.

I do not know who decided to play 'It's All Over Now, Baby Blue' as Dudley was carried out at the end of the service, but I was not the only one who heard the line where the recording faded in. 'Look out, the saints are coming through', sung Bob Dylan, as his coffin went by us. He was the teacher who had made poetry and life meaningful and made us somehow more alert to it again.

His death brought strange reactions among the poets in the department too. Philip Terry wrote an uncharacteristically conventional, loose poem about the loss of people like Dudley from the world of teaching. It contained a reference to the Dylan resonance above, and protested that 'We are no longer free to think, as you were / mixing farming and scholarship in a wild dance'.

The word 'scope', quoted above from Shakespeare's sonnet 29, in 'Desiring this man's art and that man's scope', seems appropriate in its shades of meaning from exactness of aim to width or range of interest. Dudley was an escape artist from narrowness of all kinds who, in his later years, accepted a monkish retreat. I feel we should have celebrated him more but, as he might have said, sometimes 'a prophet is not without honour, save in his own country, and in his own house' (Matthew 14:57).

If you want to know what Dudley looked like, imagine the Lee Marvin character in the film *Cat Ballou* (1965) – but sober and intellectual. He liked the comparison when I mentioned it to him. He had presence. The world seemed a more significant place and the possibility of holding life and poetry seriously was never absent. There are many stories I could add about him – and they were all his work, too.

I always told him I was still his student and that is true again now. Dudley always had something new, rooted in the ancient, to tell us 'the oldest, yet the latest thing'. We suffer from intellectual agoraphobia these days. When I mentioned feeling anti-intellectual to him, he said, 'I'm *post*-intellectual', adding, 'You can have that one for free'. His best writing, like his best teaching, was never less than life-enhancing and sought to heal the world.

2. Dudley and Dionysus: unpublished

I used to ask Dudley about his past and I remember him telling me about his time at Cambridge, where he studied for an MA and began his PhD about Yeats. Around this time, new thinkers and Cambridge contemporaries like Germaine Greer were publishing influential books, such as *The Female Eunuch* (1970). He told me that he had, even then, gone so far as to contemplate a book about Dionysus and that there was interest from publishers in this project. He said, only part joking, that Dionysus came to him in a dream or vision and forbade the book. Was this just a Dionysian ambiguity, from the messenger of the god of ambiguity, in a 'now you see him, now you don't' move characteristic of his strange and ungraspable qualities? I wasn't sure but was happy with the mythic tale of the ultimate mythic mystery.

Later, Dudley gave lectures on *The Bacchae* by Euripides, which remained on the first-year reading list, despite students and some teachers finding it too baffling and irrational – which, arguably, it is. One of his central, profound and salient observations about this Greek tragedy was that it provided a kind of 'inoculation' against the kind of violence and disorder it depicted. This still seems a useful point and provides anyone with a reason to take it seriously. Dudley was always serious, even in comedy, and he consistently asked of the literature he taught that it be interrogated for its seriousness.

Dudley's colleague in myth, Leon Burnett, recently revealed that he had some chapters from what seemed to be an unpublished book on Dionysus. I call these chapters *Where Is Dionysus?*, which was the title of a talk Dudley once gave. I remember he was working on this project when he retired, but that he had put it aside later, wondering whether anyone would be receptive to it.

Leon sent me at least half a book and is actively seeking for further chapters among Dudley's files. Although, disappointingly, there was nothing of the Cambridge academic intrigues around Jane Harrison he had mentioned in the 'Where Is Dionysus' talk to be seen for now, the extant chapters were much like, in places, Dudley's Primitive Mythology class.

I hope the rest of the book is around somewhere. In the meantime, the quality of Dionysus to vanish, to escape confinement, to be half-there, half-gone and yet more present than any other god, or God, not only seems most appropriate to their mysteries, but also to Dudley himself. As Phil Terry said to me in an email, 'half a book by Dudley sounds good'.

Even in just the introduction and chapters one, six, eight, nine and eleven, we have around 35,000 words of very readable work on Greek literature and ritual. The tone is more considered and sober than Dudley when he was speaking in his heyday, but the quality of the writing and his usual virtues are there. Chapter one sees the author proclaim himself 'the priest of Dionysos' (his preferred spelling). Chapter six, on Persephone, is unique, like a deeper version of a similar class from Primitive Mythology. Chapter ten states perhaps his main theme here: 'Dionysos withdraws into the shadows, and Athenian greatness is gone forever'.

Another central theme of Dudley's, from the same chapter:

The lens of mythic speculation makes events both more and less real: less real in the obvious sense that a mythic event, being 'made up', never took place, but more real in that, if powerfully and simply constructed, it can enter the soul of the beholder as something more important than a historical happening could be because it expresses a permanent, hence forever-repeatable truth about human being.

By the time we get to chapter eleven, Dionysus and his prophet Teiresias are 'in retreat' and the book seems more about Greek tragedy, and how it might apply to, or be a warning about our own times.

As Dudley says in his introduction: 'Perhaps the major obstruction to acquaintance with Dionysos is that he wears so many hats...' and, from the same paragraph: 'Dionysos is the god whose coming we are likely to resist'. From later in the introduction: 'Of course all the gods come and go, but it is the speciality of Dionysos, his hallmark, as one might expect of the god who began as keeper of the seasons.' Connected to this is the undying quality of the agricultural god of death and rebirth, as Carl Kerényi indicated in the subtitle of his book *Dionysos* (1976), who here is 'the archetypal image of indestructible life'.

Again, back in class, Dudley would do a whole session on Tennyson's 'Ulysses' (1842), and the undying seeking of the 'undiscovered'. The lines that come to mind are these: 'Death closes all: but something ere the end, / Some work of noble note, may yet be done, / Not unbecoming men that strove with gods.' This makes 'Look out, the saints are coming through' now sound like a rising up: a rebirth.

Two Poems

JOHN FULLER

'Meditation'

Sunlight in a sitting-room, memento
Of an afternoon's longueur, when Mme. Monet,
Positioned on a canapé, is pleased
To become paint, till so much time's elapsed
While he adjusts the details and design
That, No, she will not wait to see it signed!
Her finger taps impatiently. She's tried
And tried, but her book calls her. She is tired
Of sitting all these hours as a statement
Of Claude's love, art's selfish testament.
Perhaps he tells her all models have aspired
To be their painters' muses, and be praised.
But she has much to do – there are the precise
Amounts required for the day's recipes,
Seeing a consommé clear or a sauce thicken
(Those strange metamorphoses of the kitchen)
And all the children's emotions superintended.
Life is a labour. It is unpredestined.
She asks herself what living will deliver,
Extemporised and not to be relived.
She's not a piece of flesh to be appraised.
She is a person, and can disappear.

The French for 'Lent' is a famous chef – Carême!
How strange. I order a *chocolat à la crème*
At a little pavement table by St. Germain
Where once philosophers, now emigrants
Debate if justice can exist on earth
And reason be acknowledged by the heart,
If love itself is more than coincidental
And common understanding non-dialectic.
This is Paris, where almost every doorbell
Leads to an atelier or bordello,
And ghosts of the 1950s in this café
(De Beauvoir's *chevelure,* the haunted face
Of Greco expecting immediate arrest,
The pensive hangdog jowls of J.-P. Sartre)
Remind me of the pathos of all exits,
Although I know that entrances exist
And those we remember have surely had their moment.
As at the Luxembourg has M. Monet
And his tender 'Meditation'. There are no
Setbacks that will keep us from pressing on.
The painter's wife turns to her novel. Night
Comes, as it will. And art is still the thing.

***

Flowers for Bees

1. Geranium
In a green shade of the garden
These untroubled flowers
Demonstrate their five petals,
Violet shading to pink
And with white at the centre.

Are they like hands reaching out
In a kind of greeting?
Are they like faces containing a joy
Transmitted in reflection?
Bees make them nod as if they are.

Although I look at them closely enough,
Glancing up frequently from my book,
I can't catch them in the act of attention
To anything beyond their own being.
These words I write are a nod of a kind.

2. Japanese Anemone
It never understood the prohibition
Of pink with yellow. It marches from its bed
On to the lawn as if it is beautiful.

But it is! Splayed stalks like a candelabra,
Large dark-veined leaves, tough and coarse.
The bees alight on it like any other.

3. Marjoram
I might have cut the marjoram for salad,
And did so, until the rainy days drove
Me indoors, and it was all forgotten.

Their little spears of green, with over-notes
Of rust or leather, are now emerald pillars
Supporting tiny clusters of pink flowers.

I counted seventeen bees upon them, delicately
Rampaging (seventeen until I could reliably
Count no more, as they circled and changed places).

I shall, I think, straddle the back of one of them,
Gripping its tigery fur, and fly away
To see where they make their honey, and to taste it.

Three Poems

SUSANNAH HART

Shining in Tampere

Are the cars still shining in Tampere?
Does Suomenlinna still rise from the sea?
Do the angles of Temppeliaukio still astonish?
Is the air still pure and are the steps
of the Russian cathedral still waiting to be climbed?
I suppose there have been other girls who ate
their prawns and their berries on trains,
other girls who fell off hired bikes when the roots
on the pine forest path surprised them,
others who sat above the town and watched
the late summer evening in its lilac settling,
trying to find the words for colour and time.
I ache for those girls, for their unspun futures,
for their rucksacks weighted with books
and their intricate simple closeness,
those long conversations that mattered so much.
There is no one else in the world but you –
I suppose you're still alive – who would understand
the cars shining in Tampere, the peeled prawns
and the sour berries, the huge mosquito bites.
We were friends, that's all. But to share so much
time with someone else is a gift, a burden,
and we gave each other those things to carry forever.
Today I met another friend we knew back then,
my friendship with her a long unbroken thread.
But it was you on Suomenlinna, you falling
from the bike, you on the top of the lilac hill,
and somewhere the thread of our friendship was broken
and we go forward carrying our heavy gifts alone.

Folklore

The past is an apple orchard. The past is rain on corrugated iron.
Remember the eggs in the kitchen garden, the gaudy apples
tumbling down the conveyor belt? The past is a sweet dark hall.

O cider farm, o bottle tops, o pink moist noses of the bulls!
O glorious rural names, those plump syllables rolling on the tongue!
Remember the garage with its single pump? Remember the apple trees?

The past is flagstones and meat hooks. The past is Bill's children.
Deep inside the story are the secrets of the plot. O heaps of rotting apples!
O prize rosettes! Remember the wedding photos in the cold front room?

O Chapman men, drovers and labourers, cowmen and apple pickers!
O women of the pantry and the range! Remember Ruby in the parlour
at The Pound? The past is mounds of yellow chicks in a Longhope barn.

Remember the cherryade and the milkfloat, the clinking of bottles
in the early summer light? The past is a cider press inside a hollow bush
where the myth took root. O my rich ripe apples! O my unforgotten fruit!

Spring onions

All the places you could be when it happens,
if it happens, all the things you could be looking at –
the empty glass on the black café table
or the flattened Coke can on the pavement by the car.
You could be chopping spring onions or deciding
between rosé and white, maybe thinking about
whether Greece would be nice next summer.
You could be choosing your latest download,
worrying about a hundred other things that might
happen, but that, as you don't yet know, will not.
And when it happens it won't be like a film or a book
or even your favourite song, but it will be a thing
all itself, a thing that makes the Coke can
or the spring onions solidify and weighten,
acquire gravity beyond their status, and afterwards,
when someone asks you about it, you will start
with the spring onions, you will remember
the acrid smell, your favourite little kitchen knife,
the flecks of mud on the green chopping board.

Concrete, Communism, Ecumenism

Dom Sylvester Houédard in the Czech Republic

GREG THOMAS

Broumov Monastery, located in the north-east of the Czech Republic just below the Polish border, is a majestic baroque complex and former monastic community. It was founded in the early thirteenth century by the Benedictines of Břevnov, based 100 miles south in Prague. By the eighteenth century Broumov had become 'a supra-regional centre of culture and education'. That's according to the catalogue for Monika Čejková's exhibition *Dom Sylvester Houédard: Endlessly Inside,* which ran at the monastery from June to October 2023. The show was part of the Ora et Lege ('pray and read') curatorial project, whose title adapts the Latin Benedictine credo 'Ora et Labora' ('pray and work').

The pieces on display by Houédard range from magnificent, rococo typewriter-art constructions creating illusions of three-dimensional depth (Edwin Morgan dubbed them 'typestracts') to 'reversible' poems, with letterforms, found objects and materials suspended in transparent sheets of plastic, designed to be viewed from both sides. Meanwhile, in the monastery's library are examples of Houédard's poetry publications, produced by his and John Furnivals press Openings. The library itself is a lavish, two-storied, barrel-shaped vault created during the early-eighteenth-century restoration that gave Broumov its current appearance. Prior to the First World War, the library contained 45,000 books, ranging from law and church history to philosophy, medicine and architecture. This collection was systematically neglected and plundered after 1945, particularly after the dissolution of the monastery by the governing Communist Party in 1950. (Returned post-Velvet Revolution to the Břevnov order, Broumov is now open to the public, though the monks never returned.)

Any Benedictine monastery is a wonderfully apposite location for a display of work by Dom Sylvester Houédard, who balanced his extravagant forays into the 1960s counter-culture and the world of intermedia art with monastic enclosure at Prinknash Abbey in Gloucestershire. It was from this unlikely base that he galvanised a group of regionally located poets and artists (including Thomas A. Clark, Astrid and John Furnival, and Kenelm Cox) into a phase of loosely collective activity animated by the idea of rendering words and language forms as visual and sonic matter. The cries of Scottish cultural nationalists aside, it is in the semi-rural south-west of England, and not in Glasgow or Edinburgh (the erstwhile homes of concrete poets Edwin Morgan and Ian Hamilton Finlay respectively), that the British concrete poetry movement, if it ever existed, found an epicentre. That was largely thanks to Houédard.

Dom Sylvester's faith and poetics were closely entwined. His work often constituted an attempt to render what I have called, in my 2019 book *Border Blurs: Concrete Poetry in England and Scotland*, a state of union with the divine. In the case of his typestracts – an extensive selection of which can be found in seconds by Googling the *sui generis* term – my own contention is that the form pushed into shape by the clacking of the typewriter keys, with its strange, architectonic appendages, its waterfalls of brackets, or its haze of commas, is not always the true object of contemplation. Rather, it is the white space, the encompassing void whose presence this curious object implies, that is the true vessel of Houédard's negative or apophatic conception of God. The *via negativa* of his poetics is also, of course, writ large in the simple use of letterforms without any semantic implication.

Houédard's work has been explored in greater depth than my own writing musters by two writers with connections to Buddhist and Catholic mysticism respectively, Nicola Simpson and Charles Verey. As Simpson writes in an article for the *Endlessly Inside* exhibition catalogue, Houédard's theological sensibilities were profoundly informed by his encounters with Buddhism during the 1960s and beyond. Based on this, she proposes 'two doorways through which the reader / viewer of this exhibition… can enter to understand Houédard's work':

> There is the direct and sudden Zen path to enlightenment invoked in a piece such as the laminate poem *live all the immediately while wafted available to the even waterlogged ground* (1967). When originally made and exhibited this was a mobile (rotating sculpture) with three petals sandwiched in red, orange and blue plastic that would have 'wafted' in the breeze made by gallery visitors circumambulating the work, a movement bringing the attentive viewer's awareness to the present moment, the now, where we can 'live all the immediately.' [….] The other doorway is through the entrance of gradual enlightenment depicted in the works that engage with the ritual practices of Tibetan Tantric Buddhism.

Simpson elaborates on this process of incremental attunement, which we are presumably able to bring to bear on a range of Houédard's work, in terms of 'performative and experiential Tantric ritual methods of mudra, mantra and yantra [which] transform the practitioner's body, speech, mind and environment into that of their chosen Tantric deity'.

The agnostic humanists amongst us might struggle with the somewhat baroque connotations of mystical experience outlined here. We might instead choose to emphasise that Houédard's engagement with Buddhism – as Simpson notes – was entirely mediated by socio-political circumstance. His work thus tells a human-centred tale alongside that of the inward path to enlightenment. In particular, the violent consolidation of Chinese control over Tibet in the 1950s, culminating in the Dalai Lama's flight from Lhasa in 1959, spread a diaspora of Buddhist monks across the west. Houédard established direct relationships with several teachers based in Britain and elsewhere as part of an interfaith dialogue committee set up in Britain under

the auspices of the Second Vatican Council (1962–5), a period of relative liberalisation and 'aggiornamento' ('bringing up to date') within the Catholic Church. It is in this context that we can frame the increasing incorporation of Zen and Tantric Buddhist symbolism into his poetics across the 1960s.

In 1950, a few years before Houédard was receiving his monastic cousins – banished by one communist regime – at Prinknash, his Benedictine brothers at Broumov were rounded up by Czecvhoslovakia's repressive communist regime and placed in an internment camp located within their own monastery and grounds. This was, the *Endlessly Inside* catalogue informs us, part of 'the first phase of the infamous Operation K – the state-controlled liquidation of male religious communities in Czechoslovakia, followed closely by Operation Ř (the dissolution of women's convents)'. All of which brings us to qualify a point made earlier in the article: while any Benedictine monastery offers an appropriate setting for Houédard's work, one located in the only former Eastern-Bloc country where an extensive concrete poetry movement emerged suggests particularly piquant routes to engagement.

In her own catalogue essay, Monika Čejková details the (fairly modest) written communication during the 1960s–70s between Houédard, a prodigious letter-writer, and three Czech concrete poets: Bohumila Grögerová, Josef Hiršal and Jiří Valoch. Čejková notes how important it was 'for artists living in totalitarian dictatorships [presumably referencing the communist Czechoslovak Republic among others] that their poems could get to foreign periodicals and exhibitions not only by mail, but often through a trusted intermediary'. If this provides some practical context for the scope of the various missives she describes – which concern exhibitions or anthologies in which one might feature the other, or list useful contacts in respective countries – it also adumbrates a brief engagement with Czech concrete poetry itself.

As Edwin Morgan wrote in his 1974 essay 'Into the Constellation: Some Thoughts on the Origin and Nature of Concrete Poetry', 'one cannot brush aside "moral, social, and psychological values" so long as the medium in question is linguistic' [here he quotes the critic Mike Weaver, who, Morgan felt, had argued too strongly for a pure, formalist variant of concrete poetry]. As evidence for the potential 'political and social engagement' of concrete poetry he name-checked the Czech concrete movement, which he described as equal to the more famous but similarly politicised Brazilian Noigandres group in terms of its 'widespread impact and distinctive qualities'.

We might see these distinctive qualities as having to do with a certain emphasis on slippage between different languages, on mistranslation and miscommunication, whereas concrete poetry in its classic iteration was often about paring down and synthesising languages – on achieving some form of transnational poetic *esperanto*. For poets working in a country that had only recently (in 1918) secured independence from the Austro-Hungarian Empire when it was overrun by the Nazi empire in 1938, and had then been co-opted as a Soviet satellite state, this emphasis on a slippage of tongues was not only anti-concrete (in the sense of being anti-minimalist, against an immaculate clarity of language) but also trenchantly political.

The most expansive period anthology of concrete poetry, Mary Ellen Solt's *Concrete Poetry: A Worldview* (1967–8), contains three works by Grögerová and Hiršal, romantic and creative partners who produced much poetry in collaboration. Two of them, 'Egotist' and 'Quarrel', consist of blocks of text in which the Czech words 'ty' and 'já' ('you' and 'I') seem to vie for control over the space. The conflict here bears connotations of lovers' tiffs, in a way which introduces gendered expression into the typologically neutral, implicitly male tonal range of the original concrete poetry movement. But the duo's third poem, 'Developer', speaks more directly to the wider socio-political realities in which the Czech concretists were operating.

'Developer' consists of two typewritten columns of capitalised letters which, through incremental permutation, morph from one word into another, or rather, into the same word in another language. Over twenty-one lines, the German 'LIEBE' ('love') becomes the Czech 'LÁSKA', while over thirty-six increments the Czech 'SVOBODA' morphs into its English equivalent, 'FREEDOM'. It's an abstract poem, but one full of oblique political symbolism. What does love signify in a coloniser's language? What does freedom mean when it expresses itself in the *lingua franca* of global capitalism? As Jamier Hilder notes of this poem in his 2016 text *Designed Words for a Designed World: The International Concrete Poetry Movement*, '[p]ost World War II Czechoslovakia was attempting to shift identities from one occupied consciousness, the German, to another, the Soviet, making the inclusion of the English word "freedom" an especially loaded political statement at the height of cold war relations'.

In short, in the context of Czech culture during the 1960s, the abdication of linguistic clarity, of semantic transparency, meant something different than it did in the spiritually loaded, non-semantic gestures of Houédard's typestracts. Crucially though, those gestures were not as divorced from earthly concerns as they might appear. In the worldview of Houédard's 'wider ecumenism', which sought spiritual truths outside the mainstream of the Catholic church in everything from Buddhism to beat culture, the stripping of semantic sense from the concrete poem was also an anarchistic gesture, one oriented towards the possible future conditions of a utopian, non-hierarchical society. As he noted in a 1966 article, 'Poetics of the Deathwish', 'merely to present the gap seems to constitute the lightest & briefest of fingers on the trigger – the least fascist invitation to engage spectator interest & participation – & so create a primitive human selfregulating society'.

These comments were not, of course, made with any focus on the Czech concrete scene, nor were they rooted in the political and cultural concerns of Houédard's Prague-based comrades. But they suggest a shared emphasis on the troubling of semantic meaning (or, indeed, its wholesale erasure) as an implicitly democratically minded gesture. It was one that could, in some cases, point mutely towards possible futures in which certain insidious systems of authority, embedded in language, have unravelled, allowing new and more humane forms of social structure to emerge in their place. This is another lesson to draw from the phantasmagorical delights on display at Broumov Monastery.

Four Poems

LAURA SOLÓRZANO

Translated by Adriana Díaz Enciso

(*delonix regia*)

The tree has died
The trunk has lived and has died
The leaves have fallen on dust
The branches sweat
The limbs' shadows and the light
(the light of the tree)
The flower of light without tree
The arboreal emotions
The avid explosions, the emotive
Branches break
A tree goes on foot like one dead

With a zombie rustle
On goes a superfluous corpse, green
Like a living corpse, rootless
The tree descends from the wind
The voice comes from vertigo
There is no light like the canopy
Nor flight like the verb
The verb comes from the tree

(from *Boca perdida*, Bonobos, Metepec, Mexico, 2005)

(sunday)

Today I experimented with colour, the faint light and absence. Some, standing, watched how the nest had dropped from the boughs.

I could feel you in the street of slanting rays that start to rebel in the afternoon and seem to be reflections from another world.

Those rays were the creatures of your distance and I scared away the memory so that the light didn't penetrate the instant when we must reach the fragile and white shell that a small bird had abandoned.

Everyone wanted to see the beginning of the violet flowering that always in these months overruns the dry boughs and looks like a blotch of faith among unleashed winds.

In that warm picture of springtime my arms would have blossomed around you.

In that family flow led by the mother, my breathing grew laboured thinking about flying off with the ideas up to that breath where our fingers, nailed to their hysteria and writing ceaselessly, would have concurred.

But we took the nest out of the thicket. We looked at the new flowers in the tree, we allowed the light to linger among us, only to think that we needed rainwater and perhaps another bicycle that might understand our grey Sunday unease.

And I, flying low, let your memory enter my fibres and fill my glass with gravidness. And an intimist pronunciation undid the times, and I thought that you were there, watching how the light, withdrawing, stayed our smiles.

(from *Nervio náufrago*, La Zonámbula, Guadalajara, Mexico, 2011)

Planet:

It had opened wide – the garden. The boughs had come to set their two feet on air. The reeds' body bent over in a joyful bow. The dragonflies pleaded to be bestowed with weight. In the open garden everything was: even the most preposterous requests blossomed or promised fruits. Desire fertilised reality. Roots bore every excess. In the growth of moss, the adventure of enshrouding everything. In the mandarin tree, a journey down the realm of scents.

It was here, in this time orchard, that the children raised in chorus the silent song, and like birds carried away the primitive elements and transformed their house.

(from *El espejo en la jaula. Antología personal,* Secretaría de Cultura, Gob. de Jalisco, Guadalajara, Mexico, 2006)

(farewell)

We went to place her inside a case and left her there (in the garden's nevermore) and locked the metal latch and left her body and left her, who was that body, because she no longer breathed my father laid flowers on the white dress and he (who had no other eyes than those) touched her hand and held it there for a bit longer, seeing the way her hair had stopped shivering, looking at the corners of her inert mouth and when my father closed the case (our agitated foliage around him) we knew what an ending is and when that ending is shut and when the farewell triumphs above everything else, we understood (as if then we could understand) that we would never see her again.

(From *Nervio náufrago*, La Zonámbula, Guadalajara, Mexico, 2011.)

Adriana Díaz Enciso writes: Laura Solórzano's poems move through multiple boundaries. They are translucent, meticulous verbal structures barely sustained on the page – they seem rather to flicker in a peculiar light. As we enter their eerie imagery we understand that this is the clear light of intellect, married to that of poetry understood as the ultimate distillation of experience. The words 'experience of the world' come to mind, not in their usual meaning of human beings as sole agents, but as world, human intellect, affections and spirit all experiencing *being* in unison. It is in the rigorous effort to give expression to this immanence that boundaries are crossed: those of verbal language and the secret language of things; of intimate human emotions spelled as manifestations of this inscrutable wholeness; of the sensuousness of the human body and of the natural world, the changing attributes of light, and the silent but no less intense inner life of the vegetal, mineral and animal realms. It is in the elusive connection of these elements that experience happens, and the poetic image that it calls for is to be found in the dislocation of language, the scrutiny of what is hidden in its hinges, the speech of the infinitesimal.

Great patience and precision are needed to unravel the laws of such poetics, and Solórzano has been liberal with both for decades, building one of the most singular – and isolated – bodies of work in Mexican contemporary poetry, the richness and beauty of which are well worth exploring.

Some Poems

WILLIAM SCOTT McKendry

Denmark Street

i.m. Lukasz Karpinski (1987–2017)

Hundreds of polytunnels are halfway to the Shetlands.
Three people killed.
Shelves clearing, according to the Met man.
Happy children sing.
What an end to the decade, Gringo.

They got you carnations, but no fennel or violets.

I can't shake the image of your final violence
going down, no doubt,
with wild panache –
one more Exquisito for the road
then, 'That's it over, folks. File out.'

They got you pansies, but no rue.

Did I ever tell you about Denmark Street?
It flooded when I was five.

We splashed in puddles, built rafts till after dark
when our brothers were sent to drag us home;
and that was the end of that, Gringo.

I can hear you going, 'What the *fuck?*'
about some client who took a photo on his phone.
Some bastard brung your favourite hat,
a Stetson type, which sat on top;
McLean near gurned, had to bite his tongue.

They got you daisies, but no columbines.

People I expected didn't turn up. Blame the storm.
I'll expect to see you bombing up the road
some morning on your bike
with your gaucho's poncho on. Gringo,
don't sneak up behind me. That's the decade done.

Beeyelzeegub

fər Jun Zɪe 7 Burnurd O Danəȝhyɪe

S'pohz Aʸ mey rohʃt ðɪs gʊes. Hėɪr'z ə pʊrpætshəl skʊelboy
spærd aɪn baʸ neys nohshənz naʸshnəl, hʊe hɪngz 'ɪmself
leyk bounti's klampɪt aɪn ækspæktėɪshyəns plenti. But noh
tėɪlər əv ɑr Iteesh wəd drɑp ə kupəl ə' Gs ən' goh, At's us naʸ,
kuz ʈhərz grafʸ needz dɪd doun ət ðə laʸngweej fæktri. Soh
yʊe mey grab ən oul Laɪngkesh hænki frɪm ʈhə byʊeəroh shælf

fər ʈhə grėɪvi sʊen laʸshən æf yər bėɪk. Hėɪr'z ənaɪr hɪng: us
frɪm ʈhɪs kwohrtər'z naʸ daft; dohn'ʸ let smohk frɪm ʈhə bohnfaʸr
fʊel yə. Aʸ'm ə cheeki bɑsdʊrd-gɪtən, but ət sʊets mə. Aʸ wəz
məkduft out ə' mə mæ'z bæli ʃtrėɪt aɪndə ʈhə tɑrmakt ʃtreeʸ
wəʈh ʈhə pɪjyənz ən' ʈhə mungrəlz ən' ʈhə gunmen ə' ʈhə waɪr
nat up sum prɪmrohz wey, soh Ә speek ʈhat Belfaʃtwa Ә hærd
frɪm ə pohrtər ɪn ʈhə Mėɪtər Infʊrmohrəm:☐Yʊe skærəd ðə kleen
fuk out ə' mee ʈhær naʸ, soh yə dɪd, kɪd, wən yə neer daʸd thær.☐

Beelzegub

'Spose I may roast this goose. Here's a perpetual schoolboy
spurred on by nice notions national, who hangs himself
like bounty's clampit on expectations plenty. But no
tailor of our *Itish* would drop a couple of Gs and go That's us *now*,
cause there's graft needs did down at the language factory. So
you may grab an aul Longkesh hanky off the bureau shelf

for the gravy soon lashin' off your bake. Here's another thing: us
from this quarter's not daft; don't let smoke off the bonefire
fool ye. I'm a cheeky bastard gettin', but it suits me – I was
macduffed out of my ma's belly straight onto the tarmacked street
with the pigeons and mongrels and the gunmen of the war,
not up some primrose way, so I speak that Belfastois I heard
from a porter in the Mater Infirmorum: 'You scared the clean
fuck of me there now, so you did, kid, when you nearly died there.'

Words from 'Beelzegub' in transl[iter]ation

I suppose I may roast this goose. Here's a perpetual schoolboy spurred on by nice notions national, who hangs himself like bounty's clampit on expectations plenty. But no tailor of our Itish would drop a couple of Gs and go, That's us *now*, because there's graft needs doing down at the language factory. So you may grab an old Longkesh hanky from the bureau shelf for the gravy soon lashing off your face. Here's another thing: us from this quarter are not daft; don't let smoke from the bonfire fool you. I'm a cheeky bastard getting, but it suits me – I was Macduffed out of my ma's belly straight onto the tarmacked street with the pigeons and the mongrels and the gunmen of the war, not up some primrose way, so I speak that Belfastois I heard from a porter in the Mater Infirmorum: 'You scared the clean fuck out of me there now, so you did, kid, when you nearly died there.'

Eejıt Phonotypes

Eejıt is a phonetic orthography befitting the Belfast Vernacular, a variety of Itish (Hiberno-English) I call Belfastwa (from the French *anglais belfastois*). It robs elements from standard and vernacular ('organic') spelling, the International Phonetic Alphabet and various other phonetic writing tradition sources. The Eejıt alphabet is as follows: a, ɑ, æ, aı, ɐ̯, ɐ̯e, b, ch {tsh}, d, ɗ, đ, e, ee {ė}, èı, ey, ə, ɔ̄, æ, f, g, ʒh, h, i, ı, j, k, {kn}, l, m, n, nk, ng, oh, oə, ou, oy, p, r, s, sh, t, t'h, th, u, ʉ, ʉe, v, w, y, z, zh, ' [glottal ʃtop].

Unless stated otherwise, Eejıt consonants correspond with those of standard written Anglo-English. Approximate North Belfast Vernacular speech sounds are noted using the 2015 version of the International Phonetic Association's International Phonetic Alphabet.

Eejıt Letter	Eejıt Example	Approx. Vernacular	Standard Written Example
ə	əbout, thə, sævrəl	ə	about, the, several,
ʉr	kʉrs, bʉrd, wʉrd, wʉr	ɜ	curse, bird, word, were
æ	skwær, swær, wær,	ɞ [ɵ] ~ ɜə	square, swear, where
ɔ̄	ınd' t̸hɔ̄ dɑrk	ə:	into the dark
a	slap, bap, wat	a	slap, bap, what
ɑ	ɑr, bɑr, ɑm, ɑr,	ɑ	are, bar, am, our
aı	t'haıt, waır, daıg	ɒ ~ ɔ	thought, war, dog
æ	sævrəl, mæni, kæt	æ	several, many, cat
i	sʉshi, bæli, mıbi	ı ~ e	sushi, belly, maybe
ı	ız, wık, klampıt	ı	is, wick, clampit
u	kuntri, huni, Hun	ʌ	country, honey, Hun
e	sez, bed, wen	ɛ ~ ɛə	says, bed, when
ee / ė	free, speek, kumpleetli	i	free, speak, completely
ʉe	tʉe, bʉets, tʉe, tyʉeb	ʉ	two, boots, too, tube
oh	boht, soh, toh, kohks	o ~ oʊ	boat, sew, toe, coax
ɐ̯	ɐ̯, flɐ̯, bɐ̯sh, nɐ̯, ɐ̯	æi ~ aı	I, fly, bash, now, eye
ɐ̯e	ɐ̯e, mɐ̯e	ɒːı	aye, ma[mm]y
èı	gèıt, Spèın, rèın, fèıs	iə	gate, Spain, rein, face
ey	sleys, wey, they	ɛi	slice, way, they
oə	poəm, oəm, floən'	oə ~ oʊə	poem, ogham, flowing
oy	choys, boy, noyz	ɔi	choice, boy, noise
ou	broun, kou, oul, snout	ɜʉ ~ əi	brown, cow, aul, snout
j	pıjyən, jam, wıjıt	dʒ	pigeon, jam, widget
zh	zhaınrə, kazhyəl	ʒ	genre, casual
nk / ng	ʃtrung, unkəl, t'hınk	ŋ	strung, uncle, think
n / kn	noh, knoh, hohl	n	no, know, hole
k	kæt, kaıf	k	cat, cough
ʒh	laʉʒh	x	lough
t'h	pıt'h, t'hurəli	θ	pith, thoroughly
th	thə, then, thoh, tɐ̯th	ð	the, then, though, tithe
ch- / -tsh	cheeki, pıtsh	tʃ	cheeky, pitch
k	kɑr	k	car
ɗ	baɗi, buɗr	t / d → ɾ	body, butter
t	tatərs	t / ɾ	tatters
đ	də rohsɟ dıs goht	t / ð → d	to roaʃt this goat
'	su'əm, u'beet	ʔ	something [sumn], upbeat
'	ən', ə', 'ımsælf	▢ [omission]	and, of, himself
ɟ / t̸h	ratɟhər'n t̸his ɐ̯	t / ð → ▢ / ʔ	ra[th]er [th]an [th]is eye

Two Poems

DON RODGERS

Mystery Tour

*Senior citizens from Shipton-under-Wychwood gather for a
photograph before setting off on a mystery tour during the
summer of 1962*

Thirty-two men and six women
assembled like a choir or squad
in front of a Leyland Leopard
expectantly facing the birdie.

By now presumably you will
each have uncovered the mystery;
or are you still journeying on,
a diaspora of dots and atoms,

one day somewhere to reconstitute
an eye, a smile, a raised hand?

Carpe Diem

Before the Appointment

Carpe Diem she said
with a grim smile
lifting a wisp of hair

from the face in the mirror
as if clearing
clouds from a drain

Winter

She heard the long shadows
whisper as they waved
from side to side

while her own shadow
starker than a tree
stretched across the frozen fields

Sunlight

The sunlight's
manner of speaking
unnerved her

not harsh
despite the occasional glare
but sidelong

the way it slid
into corners
ousting shadows

Ave Maria

Like a bird
as blue as happiness
aglow in candlelight

how softly she sang
to the head in the nest
of sticks and stones and spider webs

Dame de Coeur

She took hold of her dear life
as if she were throttling
a Dame de Coeur

watched in anguish
as one by one
the red petals fell

Three Poems

DAVE WYNNE-JONES

Yin and Yang

I imagine Li Po's old lady
haunting him;
coming round corners
in the middle of a lyric,
asking awkward questions,
complaining, condemning,
with him trying this way and that,
losing all affectation, all
cleverness, becoming
simple as a sunrise
letting light fall on high snows,
reflecting upon a cascade between crags
in the middle of Wu mountains,
haunted by moonlight's watery embrace,
of one mind at last with that old lady.

Leonard and the Darkness

So, Mr Cohen, you have finished
your long conversation with G-d
who, after all the hallelujahs,
is and is not love,
gives and takes away,
that, 'I am that I am',
an answer and not an answer,
sounding perplexed, plaintive even
(minus the obligatory thunderclap)
as any narcissist might on his deathbed.
Yet, though He let the Nobel committee
get it wrong, put out the light,
and cut you off mid-sentence,
it was still you who had the last word.

On Shakespeare's Sonnet 130

Your poem's for every man who's found his woman's
Nail clippings littering the bathroom floor,
Pubic hairs coiled like springs in the washbasin,
Or removed from the bath a plug of her long hair,
But more for every man who's ever kissed
His lover's stretch marks, woken to her snoring,
The cellulite of thickening thighs caressed
Or stroked her hair, greying now and thinning;

Or for old lovers who have loved beyond
The limitations of idealisation,
Wiped noses, bottoms, chins of those beloved
Who cannot now conduct a conversation;
Tough love, caring despite decay or pain
Of loss, loving with eyes wide open

A View of England

The poetry of Philip Pacey

JEREMY HOOKER

Fifty years ago, shortly after my son was born, the poet Philip Pacey and I walked over the Sussex Downs, sleeping out one night under a harvest moon. Philip recorded the experience in his poem 'Walking the Sussex Downs'. He captured the heat of the days and the toil and pleasures of our walk in the poem. But 'Walking the Sussex Downs' is more than merely descriptive, since his way of looking constitutes a vision of downland that is at once immediate and traditional. Paul Nash was one of the artists we talked about, and Philip's image of a field of flints calls Nash to mind:

> where this field ends
> or seems to end, in our vision
>
> another begins. The flints in its
> tight furrows mere specks to these
> all-downland-contracted-to-a-stone
>
> prodigious ploughwreckers before us, pitted
> with hollows, knobbled with hill-forts
> and tumuli.[1]

Samuel Palmer was another painter we talked about on that walk in 1974, and we were alive to the tradition of art and literature associated with the pastoral world around us. Thinking of this now, in the light of Pacey's later poetry, especially *Charged Landscapes* (the sequence of poems published by Enitharmon in 1978), I can see that from one point of view he may be described as a neo-romantic poet – that is to say, a poet close in spirit to the artists, such as Nash, John Piper and David Jones, who revealed the expressive power of British landscape, rich in history and myth, and representing the identity of particular places. In Pacey's case, this means that he both values the picturesque and is keenly aware of its limitations. Always a lover of the natural world, his 'view of England', which in 'Walking the Sussex Downs' opens on the 'spaciousness' of downland, embraces geology, the industrial and pre-industrial, and the urban present. The process common to nature and the works of human beings is making, creativity, so that while his 'scenes' are rendered in exquisite detail they invariably convey the physical effort that has produced them.

The 'Wilmington' poem in *Charged Landscapes* begins:

> As the shadow of a cloud is
> blown from the downs, out leaps the Long Man!
> With a stave in each hand poised

to take off down the hill's slope
up and over the Weald. On the edge
of an energy never yet used up,

> though in moments that moment seems
> imminent.

The poet is, as it were, surprised into vision at moments when he perceives an energy in the land, which seems, like the Long Man, to leap out at him. At 'Cwm', after arguing with his companion, he says: 'we stop, to let the place / work on us'. Discoveries of overlooked places, and self-discoveries, characterise these vital poems, which have nothing to do with conventional 'beauty spots'. In 'Oldham Edge', for example:

> sulphurous skies, between black
> flat-based cumulus, the bleak scarp
> of the Pennine Range, Lancashire, in shadow
>
> but for sun smiting sand-blasted steeples,
> unsealing occasional green; gleaming from,
> not absorbed by, wet roofs of terraces.

What the poems 'unseal' is a working relationship between the human and the outer world, releasing what in 'Scotland' Pacey calls 'A landscape's charge / imprisoned, like identity / till a human reflects it'.

Falling into Place is a generous selection of Pacey's poetry which draws on several books and a number of pamphlets. The first poem comes from his time as a student at Cambridge in 1967, the last poems – as they will sadly be, for Pacey is now suffering from dementia – are three delightful 'Owl Poems' (2021). His early poems were included in *Dragon,* the student magazine of the University College of Wales, Aberystwyth. These were written in the period when we first met, when I was a lecturer at the university and Pacey was studying art librarianship at the College of Librarianship Wales. The editor of the selection, Daryl Runswick, generously describes me as his mentor. I must gently correct this by saying that, as young poets, we were comrades, supporting each other and sharing enthusiasms and discoveries.

Among the latter was Ronald Johnson's *The Book of the Green Man* (1967). This might be described as a lyric discovery of England and Wales by an American poet, who brought to native sources, such as Wordsworth and Henry Vaughan, Delius and Kilvert, a poetic art influenced by William Carlos Williams and Ezra Pound, which makes extensive use of quotations. Gary Snyder was another poet who appealed strongly to both of us, as, in the case of Pacey, is testified by his early, prize-win-

---

1 Philip Pacey, *Falling into Place: Selected poems 1967–2021*, ed. Daryl Runswick, Dal Segno Press, 2022, p. 114.

ning long poem 'James L. Maxim and the Paved Causeway over Blackstone Edge'. Use of written and other 'found' materials is a technique Pacey has occasionally employed over the years, as in 'Lostock Fox' and 'A Priest to Us All'. The latter is 'for my father', a Methodist Minister who had a profound influence on Pacey, both for his keen perception and enjoyment of nature, and because he honoured but was unable to share his faith. Pacey's philosophy of Love, which emerges ever stronger as the poems face up to an endangered world, might be described as a secular version of his father's belief.

Charged Landscapes is a vivid, confident sequence of poems, and a major achievement. When it first appeared I wrote about it in a piece called 'Landscape of Fire', which emphasised its dynamic quality.[2] In this still quite early work, Pacey has mastered his expressive speaking voice combined with flowing lines. The opening of the first poem, 'Uffington', provides an example of the fluidity that characterizes the sequence as a whole:

From the eye of the Uffington White Horse
the downs' every feature: Spur, combe,
and fluting; lifted by low sun

waves of a fossil sea, surging again
as wind through barley, breaking
on Berkshire's Plain.

Among the many other places celebrated, including Devon, Lancashire, London, Wales, Scotland and Yorkshire, is 'Wittenham Clumps', '*after Paul Nash*'. In a note on the sequence Pacey says: 'The Charged Landscapes... seek to enact "sometimeses", in which, as Paul Nash put it, "the light shines thro" the visible world and charges it with significance. A charge is a force which travels back and forth between two points which it connects... in these poems it is the space between Nature out there, and human nature, which is charged'. As well as referring to Nash, 'charged' also invokes Gerard Manley Hopkins's 'The world is charged with the grandeur of God'. It follows from this sense of things that Pacey's poems record experiences of the numinous, and are often about processes of making and doing, where inner and outer, mind and landscape, connect.

Another Hopkins image, 'earth's eye' from 'Ribblesdale', haunts a number of Pacey's poems and provides the title of one collection. 'And what is Earth's Eye, tongue or heart else, where / Else, but in dear and dogged Man'. The line encapsulates a vision, which Pacey, in his way, develops, connecting mind and feeling with nature, and emphasising Man's doggedness, his persistence as what David Jones called 'Man the maker'. Looking, in this context, is always more than seeing. It is a fully embodied sense, and 'Earth's Eye' perceives a vision of what is real. Thus, the opening of 'Charged Landscape: *Uffington*', quoted above, implies not a picturesque view, but a creative energy, as if the White Horse is engendering the landscape it is part of.

2 Published in *PN Review* Vol. 6 No. 3, and reprinted in *Poetry of Place*, Carcanet Press, 1982.

It follows from this sense of things that Pacey's poems are often about active processes. He is a poet who finds inspiration in walking, as well as a man who uses his hands and who appreciates others doing the same. Two of his most memorable poems are 'The Axe Masters' and 'On Reading "The Wheelwright's Shop"'. In 'The Axe Masters' he is most like David Jones in his relish for things, natural and man-made, their textures and colours: axes 'pale grey green or blue-grey / fine-grained volcanic ash, ground / granite hard between the millstones / of moving mountains'. The 'thingliness' of the axes is closely related to the geological processes that produced their material and to the geographical journeys of their distribution. The poem inspired by George Sturt's book expresses a similar relish for the work of later craftsmen, 'understood but partially by each' in the part that's his, partaking of // the thing itself through love'. Here, the tradition of Ruskin behind Pacey's neo-romantic sensibility is plain to see.

From the beginning, Philip Pacey, excited by the work of David Jones and of the American Black Mountain poets, has been an experimental poet. This is nowhere more evident than in the collection *In the Elements Free* (1983), reproduced in its entirety in this selection. Spacing of words and lines on the page is the principal feature of these poems, with the aim of enacting the processes that are their subject, such as 'Building Dams', 'Flying Gliders' and 'Waving to Trains'. They are physical poems, enactments of doing and making, which also adapt or embed quotations from other texts, including Hopkins and *Four Quartets.*

The collection that follows, *If Man* (1984), also reproduced in full here, is formally very different, exchanging the freedom of the previous collection for tightly organized short poems. These are characterized by tension, both formal and emotional. *If Man* constitutes a significant sequence of modern religious poems. The title refers to Josephus's words from *The Antiquities of the Jews*: 'Now there was about this time Jesus, a wise man, if it be lawful to call him a man, for he was a doer of wonderful works – a teacher of such men as receive the truth with pleasure'. Admiring yet sceptical, Josephus raises the question of Jesus's humanity. And this is the focus of Pacey's poems, in which Jesus experiences Creation 'from the inside', and wrestles with 'the human condition', which he is 'in': 'I also have a death / to contend with, have to wrest / my best self from doubt / and ease'. 'Jesus Walking' says of himself: 'who I am, human, permitted / only momentary openings onto, knowings of / God whole'. The poems do not deny transcendence, but their emphasis is on the earthly, as in the treatment of Jesus as a human child, who has 'brought love to a world / love is not absent from'.

First and last, Pacey's poetry is concerned with the real. Lines from *If Man* spell this out: 'O Man, drawn / by the eternal in things, not to own / what is real is not easy'. His work is both illuminated by a sense of the numinous, especially in landscape, and troubled by 'the God problem'. Above all he is concerned with 'hallowing', in the words that Martin Buber used as epigraph to *Charged Landscapes*: 'Nature needs Man for... its hallowing'. *On Being Incarnate* is a later collection, published in 2007 by the Scottish poet Duncan Glen, his friend and colleague at Preston Polytechnic. The title signifies a key theme in Pacey's work, and my sense is that Pacey, as he develops as a poet and a father in the nuclear age, in an endangered world, allows himself, with courage, to become more vulnerable. He speaks of 'the poems I'm writing / as my building nuclear shelters', and his belief in love as the ultimate value encounters grief at the death of family and friends and his own declining health. It is a delight, then, to find such vitality in his last poems, which greet owls in the garden tree with resilience and humour, and sheer appreciation of their real being:

Our owls it seems can deviate at the last second
from their original path

to correct their trajectory –
no longer heading straight at us
behind the bedroom window

as if summoned by my wife's rag and bone man cry
'Any old owls?', her uncanny knack
of judging the gloaming and dawn light just right.

Three Poems

IMOGEN WADE

Pilates Workout Monologue

The carpet is soft under my back.
I am slick as a Calypso lolly stick.
Lower my spine; exhale to bridge;
back down. What advice would I
give myself – if I was not myself?
I used to love nothing better than
being wrong. Babies are born all
the time; not a single one is mine.
I practice contralateral twists with
breath control, thoracic rotations,
pelvic tilts, spine flexion. Sunday's
workout will be chest flys, narrow
squats, bicep curls. My final goal
is to raise my grief over my head
like a hundred kilogram kettlebell.

Meditations on Intimacy

It is, I must admit, a surprise to see you here.
I thought the robin might have taken you
but your lungs are still wheezing.

I used to walk down by the river,
even when it got dark early in the winter.
For all I know, you were one of the men I passed
in the blackest December.

Years fell forwards like drunk girls
on pavements;
we didn't catch a single one.

Commonality is a form of intimacy,
like being born in the same hospital or both loving
Brie. I feel closer to you than ever before.

At opposite ends of a long dining table,
the kind you see in stately homes, we shared
our time apart like a meal.

Horror

I imagine what my jewellery will look like
a hundred years from now, when I'm not around
to wear it. Too cheap to pass down. Landfill?
Grave? Just – lost – the way some things are
in mysterious ways? The piskie earrings;
the locket; the fake pearls. Lost things all live
somewhere. So I imagine what my jewellery
will look like in a hundred years – tarnished
bracelet without a wrist; soil-encrusted ring
without a finger; my baubles floating in water.

Four Poems

SARAH WIMBUSH

Scargill

i
The dictionary is his Bible. Full stop.

He knows boys who were crushed
with only a handful of adjectives in their tipple tins.

Some words shall always be difficult to pronounce:
Oaks, Huskar, Senghenydd.

ii
He points at the dole-not-coal paddy train,
it will arrive shortly at Platform Do-or-dinosaur.

Rule 41, rules okay, he says
the National Executive Committee says.

Inky corridors begin to infect conservatories.

There could be other words, other skies
but his eyes – blue and infinite – have limitations,
there's one path lads: picket!

iii
Faces crowd into a crown.

Each step up the mountain creaks like a blue back.

He lights the wall of a stadium with his cap lamp,

the stray-dog-kids are coming, he says,
raises his iambic voice, that finger.

Berry Hill

Brothers, when did this wound
redden between us?
We are not simply *Notts in our blood* –
I'm from Castlecomer, he's from Ukraine.

Don't manride into our town pointing
your headboards and ballyrags
like it's Towton – this descent
into Michael Fletcher and the Krays.

Can't you feel the layers
of neo-liberal chaff forming a scab,
now an island. And lads, look, see,
the black picket fence – it's smiling.

Closure

Boulders ebb to shingle
on the pithead.
Washed ashore
they will blister
and dissolve
into a kingdom
of white dwarfs.
A dusty old gull flaps
above the closed shop
as if to say, *I told you so,*
and the earth
will meet itself again
and seams shall fall
back to sleep.
And the cutters' chatter
is retold as a pickaxe,
and happy misery lives
in a can of Special Brew.
And the city commissions
an art installation
out of steel-toe caps
and Davy lamps.
And we will watch
their manhood's
dangle before us
on meat hooks,
a marble stare
on each coal face.

Coal Kid

Who knitted that jumper?

Do you sleep in it and what colour
are those words?

Who is the good boy walking behind you?

When did the sole begin to come away
on your shoe?

Were you hand-painting earlier or riddling coal?

Is it acceptable to say emaciated in front of a boy?

How many lost boys does it take to eat
a bag of scraps?

Have you ever had a dream?

Will there be extra beans for doing the chippy run?

Did Thatcher pin this picture on her fridge?

Trick question: how many boys died
down Markham Main?

Stones, do your eyes feel like stones?

Does the wool itch like a cloak of dead shrews?

Why can't you look at me, boy?

Reviews

Not I

Ned Denny, *Ventriloquise* (Carcanet) £12.99
Reviewed by Michael Edwards

The title of this exceptional work is given unsearchable depth by an epigraph from St. Paul: 'I am crucified with Christ: nevertheless I live; yet not I, but Christ liveth in me'. *Ventriloquise* examines the ways in which this *not I* may be found, and may speak in poetry, beginning with the crucified self – 'Each bared morning is a fine time to die' – as it contemplates the creation and is disturbed by continually hearing the 'one re-re-repeated Word'. How, in his poems, can the poet be, not impersonal but at once there and not there? How can he become 'the one who knows how / to keep silent in song'?

The answer is partly through a particular form of translation, something that the opening poem brilliantly exemplifies. Its first part offers three versions of the same passage in the *Tao Te Ching*, not by Denny but by three other translators. Its second arises from a phrase attributed to Aeschylus by Maurice Blanchot. Above all, while these sources are acknowledged, the whole poem is silently ventriloquized by William Carlos Williams, whose triplet form steps down sure-footed across the page. Translations are already revealing in this perspective, since they belong to no one, and Denny goes further by *trans-lating* the originals, carrying them across to his view of reality. By small touches, he opens Baudelaire's 'L'Invitation au voyage' to the world as continually falling and yet as continually being plunged 'in glory'.

To show the fallen and falling world Denny calls on Chénier, Ronsard and others, in versions usually updated by contemporary idiom and explicitness, and especially on Heine, whose 'Götterdämmerung' he transforms into a street-wise satire of our own accelerating twilight. These descents into unremarked depths of our condition are often redeemed, however, by shards of light. The penultimate poem, whose rocking anapaestic-iambic beat recalls parts of Eliot's *Sweeney Agonistes*, has its sharp, enjoyable satire framed by a Dantean epigraph on the age beginning anew and justice returning and by a bird singing *'dawn wield your gold'*.

That dark world is named as 'Civitas Diaboli'. The 'Civitas Dei' is represented in 'Chattels', a major and moving poem on what it means to be in the world but not of the world – to be already in the City of God. It transfigures well-worn expressions: the speaker lives in 'a glorified / shed', where 'glorified' recovers its full meaning, and walks on 'threadbare flying carpets', where 'flying' hints at the supernatural in the natural. 'Shed' and 'threadbare' characterize the speaker as 'a person of no importance'. This phrase is in 'Reading', another 'translation' which, via T'ao Ch'ien, at once suggests the superiority of nature to whatever we make of it – 'The meadow-grass has grown taller than the mind' – and the poet's ability to renew it in the imagination – 'trees like green lions shimmy in the slightest wind'. Poetry is thereby 'kenning what's real': both knowing it thoroughly and finding a language of true and re-creative periphrasis.

Metaphors, always surprising and full of meaning, also abound: 'pavements a light / rain has made fathomless', while a number of perfect haikus both offer moments of sudden illumination and show the zen-like nature of Christian glimpses of a kind of timeless now.

In a sense, the poet always ventriloquizes, by arranging the poems that mostly *come*, from who knows where, into the changed and partly surprised voice which speaks to us from his book. Denny has explored and refined this process in each of his works. By looking close and listening hard, you discover a new and very remarkable poet. He is a real find. Find him.

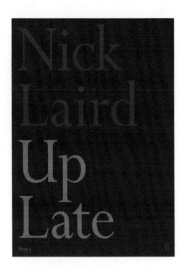

Fuckety fuck

Nick Laird, *Up Late* (Faber) £14.99
Reviewed by Harry Sanderson

Nick Laird publishes a new collection at the rate of around two a decade: *To a Fault* (2005), *On Purpose* (2007), *Go Giants* (2015), *Feel Free* (2018). The titles follow a pattern of clipped, ambiguous syntax. What should we make of *Up Late*?

The 'late' is clear. The book opens with the poem 'Grief', and proceeds on that theme. The title poem, which takes up the entire second section, is a prolonged elegy for Laird's late father. Even when not working directly in elegy Laird's approach is inflected with mourning. In 'The Outing' he finds a magpie pecking at a dead rabbit on the lawn and reflects that he will return to a house 'a little different; harder, sharper / and where my children will not look at me'. In 'Pac Man' his daughter lets go of a balloon and he finds it 'Odd to watch the realisation take, up close, / like this, the central lesson of one-way loss'. Elsewhere he simply seems depressed; sitting on a bench in the square he finds 'Everything already is fraying at the edges if not completely gone. Everyone / is mourned in turn...'.

The collection is bookended, with Laird declaring in the final poem 'I put away my grief'. As in his titles, we should be wary of taking that pronouncement at face value. While Laird might be proposing his collection as a therapeutic, he may just as well be shooing his sorrow away, or locking it up for later: everywhere the poems suggest that loss is inchoate and inescapable, with mourning the only available pastime.

What about the 'Up'? This is not a nocturnal collection – much of it is set in the sun. Rather, it might refer to Laird's ability to find a lyrical intensity within otherwise ordinary phenomena. The elegies here are imbued with the kind of frisson that Laird typically draws out from everyday experience, so that grief is lit up like a painting in a dark church.

Partly this occurs on a formal level. As in *Feel Free*, he moves away from the more traditional verse forms of his early collections, so that metre generally haunts less regular lines. In the longest prose piece – elegising a cancer patient – he does not abandon sound:

The hair of the Green Man looking out at our knees is made of delicately carved leaves, and he has apples for cheeks, and when Eddie says touch wood, and we do, we are communing with trees that stood here once and will again.

Above all he is preoccupied with how much difference he can fix in familiar words, at one point proposing 'heaven' as the past particle of 'heave'.

Part of this luminosity must be an acknowledgment of art's uneasy representation of loss. The reconciliation of sorrow within any aesthetic must give it meaning, so that an elegy can never reflect the emptiness of its source: the poem is inevitably 'up' even when the subject is late. In the title poem, Laird hurls himself against the conditions of the stanza, in and out of pentameter:

Alastair Laird is dead. Fuckety fuck. Fuckety
fuck fuck fuck fuck. My dad is dead. Bad luck.
The light breaks and the night breaks and the line
breaks and the day is late assembling.

As in Douglas Dunn's *Elegies* (1985) or Mary Jo Bang's *Elegy* (2007), the collection is both a gesture of love and a cry for help, defined above all by the desire to put a death mask on tragedy.

The collection's most heartbreaking poem, 'Attention', addresses a friend with a terminal brain tumour. It ends with the image of Michelangelo hurling a hammer at his own sculpture of Moses because he loved it so much and 'cried that it would not speak'. Laird's poems cannot enliven his subjects, not really, a truth which gives the book sympathetic tension. In 'American Poem', he questions the formula:

I know nothing of your grief, granted,
Nor you mine, but isn't that why we're here?

The question offers the possibility of poetry as a viable coping mechanism. For now, it's enough.

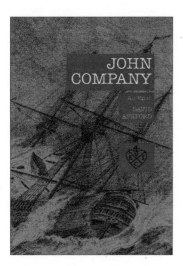

Monstrous Epic

David Ashford, *John Company, An Epic* (Pamenar Press), £16
Reviewed by Paul Ingram

From experimental publisher Pamenar Press, *John Company, An Epic* by David Ashford is at once an exuberantly ambitious book-length epic poem, a sustained exercise in textual collage and an immanent critique of the consciousness of empire. The protagonist of the work is the East India Company, personified with the familiar sobriquet 'John Company'. This personhood, however, is principally legal rather than literary. The EIC is not, by means of a rhetorical device, magically made relatable or given a human face. It remains fundamentally inhuman, a *persona ficta* that stands in on paper for an evolving complex of commercial, administrative and military operations. Over twelve sections totalling some two hundred pages, Ashford's 'John Company' is figured less as an epic hero, more as a kind of monster – hybrid in form, many-headed, fire-breathing.

Definitionally, the EIC is difficult to pin down – mercantile in orientation, but fulfilling functions of a state; part-capitalist enterprise, part-territorial power. Technically it was an English joint-stock company established by Royal Charter in 1600, with a monopoly on trade in the Indian Ocean region. In its heyday, the EIC was the most powerful corporation in the world, dominating a vast area encompassing much of the Indian subcontinent as well as parts of Southeast Asia and East Asia. It commanded armies, levied taxes and minted coins, increasingly acting as a de facto colonial administration, prior to the direct rule of the British Raj in India. Disempowered by an Act of Parliament in 1858, the EIC was eventually dissolved as a legal entity in 1874.

Properly epic in scope, *John Company* spans the whole two-hundred-and-fifty-year period, beginning with 'The Act of Incorporation':

> Wee doe erect, make, ordaine, constitute,
> establish, and declare by these Presents,
> and that by the same name of Governour and Company
> of Merchants of London trading into the East-Indies,
> they shall have succession...

Foregrounding the piratical origins of the venture, Ashford charts the early voyages undertaken in its name, on ships evoking suitably mythic-classical associations: the *Dragon* and the *Hector*. The expansive account that follows covers the EIC's dealings with the Mughal Empire; competition with its great rival the Dutch East India Company; consolidation of its control over Indian affairs; and episodes in other locations including Japan and China. The plot is full of incident; the events depicted have inherent historical interest. Yet *John Company* is far from a straightforward narrative history, and neither is it a conventional epic poem, notwithstanding the many allusions to that tradition.

The book is based on impressive archival research and makes a singular contribution to the literature on this topic. It is distinguished by its experimental poetic form, a decidedly modernist (or late-modernist) take on the epic, which employs documentary-montage techniques developed by Ezra Pound, William Carlos Williams and others. Ashford raids the letters and written testimony of various envoys, agents and functionaries of the EIC. These primary sources are incorporated into the poem, in open-form verse that snakes across the page. The individual speakers collectively approximate the eponymous figure, whose nature is suggested by the characteristics they have in common.

They share a preoccupation with quantification, obsessively detailing amounts, dimensions and distances, listing goods and totting up prices:

4 Bookes fine Calico	rials 024. —
1 Tapseele	rials 007. —
1 Simmian Chauter	rials 008. —
5 li. Allowayes Socotrina	rials 010. —

There are similar lists of commodities, materials, weaponry, livestock, buildings and so on – another echo of classical epics, in which such enumerations, for example of riches or gifts, frequently recur. In *John Company*, these blocks of text are by turn alienating and immersive. As the inventories proliferate, the overriding impression, apart from the sheer volume of stuff, is of a relentless cataloguing, classifying intelligence. Objects are sorted into categories, measured in definite units and presented as in principle exchangeable. The world is treated reductively as so much data, to be itemised and ordered according to an impersonal, top-down system. This quantitative cast of mind ultimately expresses the inhumanity of a capitalist-cum-colonial logic that subordinates the needs of human beings to the pursuit of profit. It might also prompt us to ask how the use of the list form in classical epics reflects the economic and bureaucratic practices of their own time.

The EIC's monstrousness is evident enough from the violence that pervades its history. It waged war continually, with both imperial rivals and local rulers. The economic regime it imposed on populations further entailed the production of poverty, disease and famine. Notoriously, the measures it took to subdue resistance extended to collective punishments, sanctioned looting and massacres of civilians. This theme runs through *John Company*, from an egregious instance of torture in Java in 1604 to bloody reprisals during the Indian Rebellion of 1857. By focusing on the ugliest aspects of the EIC, Ashford refutes the currently resurgent apologism that seeks to minimise the crimes of British imperialism.

This results in some of the most impactful passages of the book, such as the chilling description of the Bengal Famine of 1770:

> I have counted them from my bed-chamber window
> in the morning
>> forty dead bodies laying within twenty yards
>> of the wall,
>> besides many hundred laying in the agonies of
>> death
>>> for want bending double,
> with stomachs quite close contracted to their
> back bones.
> I have sent my servant to desire those who had
> strength,
>> to remove father off...

The scene becomes more gruesome still, with jackals and vultures descending on the bodies of the dead. The extremity of the imagery contrasts with the sometimes dry, legalistic-bureaucratic tone. This manner is maintained even in the face of such horrors, as the speaker carefully notes the number of corpses and their distance from the wall. Indeed, the horrifying effect may be heightened by the inappropriate register. At the same time, the reader is manoeuvred into the position of a detached observer, who is nevertheless implicated in what unfolds. The vantage point of the bedchamber and the interposition of the servant convey that pretended separation, as well as a deeper complicity.

Typically, this compromised perspective is the only one made available to us. For the most part, Ashford immerses us in the discourse of the perpetrators, constructing his collage out of their repurposed words, which are cut up and combined to disclose the contradictions of the ruling ideology. Other languages, signs and symbols are integrated into the elaborate design as untranslated fragments, emphasising their alienness from the point of view of the colonising culture. We might interpret this as a critical reflection of the historical record itself, which is similarly skewed by the weight of documentary evidence originating from the EIC. Its voice, backed up by extensive records, is seemingly inescapable. That inescapability is explicitly thematised in *John Company*.

The poem creates a claustrophobic atmosphere, confining us to a consciousness united, in the end, by nothing but cold calculation and pervasive violence. It does not shrink from the facts, while going beyond mere documentation to impress on the reader, as something directly experienced, the inhumanity of the protagonist, essentially by trapping us inside his head. In this light, *John Company* recalls the dictum – adapted from another modernist pioneer of documentary-montage techniques – that history is a nightmare from which we are trying to awake. A strikingly original work, Ashford's monstrous epic emerges out of the depths of that nightmare.

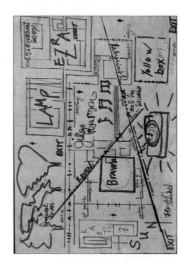

Sonic Bricolage

Jasmina Bolfek-Radovani, *Knitting Drum-Machines for Exiled Tongues* (Tears in the Fence) £9.99
Reviewed by Oliver Dixon

Multilingual poetry is not a recent innovation. The macaronic verse of medieval Europe playfully combined vernacular and Latin elements for humorous or satirical intent, whereas in Classical Persian poetry, *maremma* (or 'speckled') poems by Rumi and Hafez mixed Persian with Arabic, Turkish and Greek words. Equally, the Modernist poetry of Pound, Eliot and Loy is sprinkled with untranslated phrases and lines from other languages, foregrounding its porous internationalism and that 'nostalgia for world-culture' which Osip Mandelstam also identified as central to his poetic project. This tendency reached its apogee in the vast macaronic melting-pot of *Finnegans Wake*, Joyce's 'collideorscope' of more than sixty languages which – while obviously not poetry – indicates both the incredible richness of multilingual cross-pollination possible to writers and the undeniable challenges it presents for readers who lack the equipment to unpack all those dizzying portmanteau-words.

Jasmina Bolfek-Radovani's poetry reflects her complex biographical and cultural heritage. Born in Serbia to Croatian and Algerian parents, and having studied in Brussels, Vienna and Uppsala before settling in London, her work is an ambitious combination of French, English and Croatian language elements, further enriched and elaborated by diverse open forms and the incorporation of visual components such as maps and photos. *Knitting Drum-Machines for Exiled Tongues* is her first collection, drawn from a period of mentorship with David Caddy. It has the added interest of being the debut publication by the imprint Tears in the Fence Books, which arises out of the excellent poetry magazine of the same name of which Caddy is editor, itself an organ with a forty-year history of bringing a diverse array of international poetry to wider audiences.

The experience of reading Bolfek-Radovani's poems can be a disorientating, defamiliarising one, as the reader's attention is pulled in so many different directions at once. Firstly, in terms of visual field, the form and layout of the poems frequently shifts between modalities, from unrhymed couplets and a ghazal to more scattered, spacious lineations and typographic experiments (eg. the fading text of 'Algerian matrix'; the dotted lines of 'Heart monologues 9'). Then there are the three languages 'structurally interwoven' to different degrees in each poem, frequently imparting a haunting, polyphonous modulation of sound-patterns across lines which seem to echo the same phrases in the different tongues, as in the plaintive 'Heart monologues 3', where the English phrases and their more comprehensible French equivalents serve to elucidate the Croatian fragments for us. In other poems, such as 'Heart monologues 11', the Croatian lines remain more opaque: apparently there is a multilingual glossary available online via a QR Code but it would have been helpful to have this as an appendix. Phonetic wordplay, the three languages jammed together with Joycean brio, works well to comic effect in 'Heart monologues 13', which almost approaches the sound poetry of Maggie O'Sullivan or Bob Cobbing.

The book's visual elements provide another layer of ambivalence and curiosity to its presentation, gesturing towards the geographical displacement inherent in the author's exilic journey. As well as the small black-and-white photos which pepper the pages, the three 'map-poems' called 'tattooed 1, 2, 3' combine place names (for example, the first map seems to depict an area of Hackney in East London) with other words and instructions ('start'; 'press enter') suggestive of a game or maze. As such, they make intriguing artefacts, but further information as to the areas being mapped and why they are being concentrated on might have brought them into sharper focus.

With so many elements of potential meaning in play, it might feel at times as though there is too much going on for the reader to get a fix on it all but there are several threads to Bolfek-Radovani's work which counterbalance this tendency towards over-determination. Firstly, as previously mentioned, there is a strong autobiographical component to the volume, with alternation between the three languages enacting the situation of being caught between different cultures, world-views and physical locations. The poem 'All that Zagreb Jazz' traces the poet's intermittent memories of Zagreb and London through her engagement with fluctuating music scenes, from New Wave to 'alternative indie' to 'ambient techno' and the jazz of Coltrane's 'A Love Supreme'. Other poems like 'The Rebirth of Sound' and 'Knitting Drum-Machines for Exiled Tongues' also capture Bolfek-Radovani's interest in electronic music and sound, both as a medium which knits together the sonic bricolage of her travels between languages and as a means of transcending the cultural disparities and sense of 'depaysement' (expatriation) she mentions in another poem.

Secondly, beyond the initially daunting complexities of her polyglot style (which one might characterise as 'metamodernist' in Furiani's sense: '*after* yet *by means* of modernism… a departure as well as a perpetuation'), there is an almost Romanticist sensibility at the core of the collection, a poignant lyricism voiced through tropes of nostalgia, longing and lost love and through often familiar imagery of hearts, nightingales and palimpsests. This imparts an emotional resonance to Bolfek-Radovani's work, an ability to confront areas of experience which cross the borders of language and nationhood by touching universal truths.

To Sing and Fly

Jesse Nathan, *Eggtooth* (Atlanta: Unbound Edition Press) $24.00
Reviewed by Susan Wheatley

In the uneasy states many of us find ourselves in now, one can't ask for more than to move with the mind of Jesse Nathan in his dazzling debut poetry collection, *Eggtooth*. Nathan, a founding editor of the McSweeney's Poetry Series, was born in California, moved to a farm in Kansas when he was child and is now back in California where he teaches.

Eggtooth is above all a book of places. Nathan's speakers encounter conflicts in, and suspended between, these places. The sound of a farmer's combine crossing bridges is 'all the speaking these roads and creeks / are wont to do with one another' ('Between States').

The title poem, 'Eggtooth', falls at the centre of the book. An eggtooth, for those like this reader who could be better versed in all things bird, is a projection on a chick's beak used by the chick to break out of its shell. 'Eggtooth' begins: 'And so at last spoke John Donne's ghost. Leaned up / out of my book and nearly bit me.' Donne's ghost urges the poet to use him as an eggtooth, 'supposing the face a blade / sustained to sing and fly'.

The first poem in the book, 'Straw Refrain', deploys a Donne-inspired stanza form while setting the reader outside in Kansas, yet also in the poet's mind. Here is the first stanza:

> Young gray cat puddled under the boxwood,
> only the eyes alert. Appressed to dirt. That hiss
>   the hiss of grasses hissing *What should*
> *What should*. Blank road shimmers. On days like this,
>   my mind, you hardly
>   seem to be.

On days like these.

The tour-de-force second section of the book is a ten-page meditation, 'Between States'. The poem confronts what 'white people'--who included the poet's ancestors--have taken from the native peoples in the 'state' of Kansas. Enough of the white settlers 'must've believed' the false but beguiling narrative that the land was home 'to a race, that long has passed away' (quoting William Cullen Bryant's 'The Prairies'). Nathan imagines 'my relatives soon flooding in / with cabinet and poppyseed'. This, even as native people 'were penned in reserves'. Meanwhile, the speaker's 'foreparents' were 'granted swaths of so-called open land / to open up'.

In a time when the impulse towards communication and comity is needed in our public life, Nathan has demonstrated that he is a poet we can pin our hopes on for many books to come.

An Act of Resistance

Harry Man and Endre Ruset, *Utøya Thereafter: Poems in Memory of the 2011 Norway Attacks* (Hercules Press) £10
Reviewed by Vik Shirley

In the foreword to *Utøya Thereafter*, the Norwegian poet Endre Ruset explains that he was already experiencing a personal loss when the tragedy occurred at Utøya Island. When the names of the victims were read out on television, it sounded incantatory, like poetry, and so Ruset began writing. Once the English poet Harry Man had joined Ruset in this project, and they were viewing the memorial gallery at Utøya, Man came up with the idea of the pattern-poems, poems shaped after photo-portraits of the victims. It is of these that the collection, based on interviews and recollections from the survivors and of the families' grief, primarily consists.

One of the poems that reflects most directly what happened on the island that 22 July reads: 'She was in between the information building and the pier. She was outside the main entrance to the café building', listing places where victims were when shot. However, what the face-form adds is more intensity to the anaphora. The repeated 'she was' is isolated twice, positioned in the centre making up the eyes and mouth of the girl. This emphasises past tense, that she has ceased to exist. Another poem reads: 'You write poems to console. A door that shuts out the rain before it. It doesn't help. No'. The 'No' is part of the word 'Nothing', which breaks and continues on the other side of the face. 'The face does' disrupts the word 'doesn't', belonging to 'doesn't go away'. Poetry can't solve, or undo, the poem is saying, but it can continue to live, even when those who are no longer with us don't. In one of the most beautiful poems, which seems so softly and delicately spoken, 'A lone violet / copper flies between trees... a speckled beauty and Reverdin's blue... a ribbon of blood, travels from flower to flower', 'the world' and 'the fact' make the eyes and face. Here the positioning illustrates the cold fact of the world in which this can happen.

'[I]n any one person is every ingredient needed to change the world', one poem reads, confirming that Man and Ruset are reclaiming both hope and beauty for the victims in this collaboration. By refusing to allow only the perpetrator's dark ugly stain to survive, the poems are an act of resistance and protest. The poems' distillation of moments and how the language is engaged raises questions: what remains when a person, in this case very young, dies in such tragic circumstances? What is poetry and what is it for? Here, it is for moving beyond the facts, beyond the perpetrator and the hate, to remember.

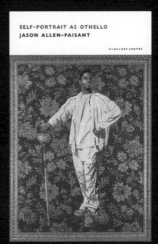

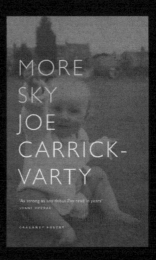

Some Contributors

Heather Treseler is the author of the forthcoming *Auguries & Divinations*, which received the 2023 May Sarton Prize, and the chapbook *Parturition*, which received the Munster Literature Centre's chapbook prize in 2020. She is Professor of English at Worcester State University. **Laura Solórzano** was born in Guadalajara, Mexico. She studied psychology and has an MA in visual arts, another in psychoanalysis. She has published ten collections of poetry and a book of short stories. Currently she teaches creative writing at the University of Guadalajara, and nurses a garden. **Don Rodgers** is a former prizewinner in the National Poetry Competition. His poems have appeared in a number of magazines and anthologies, and two collections of his poetry have been published by Seren. As well as poetry, he has written for the radio and for six years wrote a weekly column on antiques for the *Western Mail*. He lives and works in South Wales. **Imogen Wade**'s poetry has been placed in competitions such as the 2023 New Poets Prize, the Foyle Young Poets of the Year Award, the Plough Poetry Prize and the Winchester Poetry Festival Prize. Her work has appeared in *The Poetry Review*. After studying English at the University of Exeter, she trained as a person-centred therapist. **James Campbell**'s memoir *Just Go Down to the Road* appeared in 2022. His latest book, *NB by J.C.: A Walk through the Times Literary Supplement*, was published by Carcanet earlier this year. **Anthony Ezekiel (Vahni) Capildeo** is a Trinidadian Scottish writer of poetry and non-fiction. Capildeo's eight books and eight pamphlets include *Like a Tree, Walking* (Carcanet, November 2021) and *The Dusty Angel* (Oystercatcher, 2021). Their interests include plurilingualism, traditional masquerade, and multidisciplinary collaboration. They are Writer in Residence and Professor at the University of York, a Visiting Scholar at Pembroke College, Cambridge, and an Honorary Student of Christ Church, Oxford. **Ned Denny** was born in London in 1975. His debut poetry collection, *Unearthly Toys: Poems & Masks*, was published by Carcanet in 2018 and awarded the Seamus Heaney Prize for Best First Collection for the following year. *B (After Dante)*, a version of the Divine Comedy, appeared in 2021. His third book, *Ventriloquise*, was published earlier this year. **Sinéad Morrissey** was born in Northern Ireland in 1972 and educated at Trinity College, Dublin. Her awards include the T.S. Eliot Prize (2013). In 2016 she received the E.M. Forster Award from the American Academy of Arts and Letters. *On Balance* was awarded the Forward Prize in 2017. She was elected a Fellow of the Royal Society of Literature in 2019. She has served as Belfast Poet Laureate (2013–14) and is currently Professor of Creative Writing at Newcastle University. She is a frequent contributor to *PN Review*. **Michael Edwards** taught at the then 'New Universities' of Warwick and Essex (where he succeeded Robert Lowell), before being elected the first British Professor at the Collège de France, Paris. He has given poetry readings and lectures in Europe, North America, Africa and the Middle East. The first Briton elected to the Académie française, he was knighted in 2014. He lives in Paris and Burgundy. **John Gallas** was born in New Zealand in 1950. He came to England in the 1970s to study Old Icelandic at Oxford and has since lived and worked in York, Liverpool, Upholland, Little Ness, Rothwell, Bursa, Leicester, Diyarbakir, Coalville and Markfield, as a bottlewasher, archaeologist, and teacher. He is a Fellow of the English Association and was 2016 Orkney St Magnus Festival poet.

Editors
Michael Schmidt
John McAuliffe

Editorial Manager
Andrew Latimer

Contributing Editors
Anthony Vahni Capildeo
Sasha Dugdale
Will Harris

Copyeditor
Maren Meinhardt

Designed by
Andrew Latimer

Editorial address
The Editors at the address on the right. Manuscripts cannot be returned unless accompanied by a stamped addressed envelope or international reply coupon.

Trade distributors
Combined Book Services Ltd

Represented by
Compass IPS Ltd

Subscriptions—6 issues
INDIVIDUAL–print and digital: £45; abroad £65
INSTITUTIONS–print only: £76; abroad £90
INSTITUTIONS–digital only: from Exact Editions (https://shop.exacteditions.com/gb/pn-review) to: PN Review, Alliance House, 30 Cross Street, Manchester, M2 7AQ, UK.

Supported by

Supported using public funding by
ARTS COUNCIL ENGLAND